THE FORLORN HOPE

THOUGHTS FROM A SUFFERING LIFE

BY BENJAMIN J. HEIDENGREN

Table of Contents

Acknowledgements

Thanks to my mother, Pattie, who pushed this book to the
point of publication.
Thanks to Janel Feldman, who first edited my horrendously
rough draft.
Thanks to Sasha Lacy, who helped me to sound much
more gracious than I am.
And
Thanks to Dan Lee for his excellent cover art.

Introduction

B efore you accuse me of hopeless heresy based on the title of this collection (judging my book by its cover), I think I ought to explain what I mean by "The Forlorn Hope".

Back in the day (think the American Revolution, the Napoleonic wars, etc. — when men fought with muskets and bayonets — the term is older than this, but I am using this particular era for the metaphor in this book), there was a limited number of tactics a military commander had at his disposal when assaulting a fortress. It most often went something like this: he would knock a hole or two in the walls with his cannon, then he would send a detachment of soldiers into those holes to breach the wall and establish a foothold inside of it, so that additional soldiers could come through in waves until they had killed or overrun all of their enemies inside the fortress.

The group of men initially sent into the breaches was called "the forlorn hope" detachment[0]. When you were sent into those breaches, you had one shot and then the short spear of the bayonet on your musket to fight an unknown (probably large) number of enemy assailants who could fire and reload as their comrades continued to fire at you. Not many people survived the forlorn hope of an assault on a heavily defended fortress. Those who did were almost always wounded or maimed.

In this life that we live, we are constantly enmeshed in a battle for the glory of God with lines drawn between good and evil. We must fight the evil and corruption in the world brought about by sin (and aided by the Devil), and we must fight the evil that lives inside us as indwelling sin. Most importantly, we must fight for the glory of God against all opponents. There are some times of rest (some), but the battle rages on and will not end until time itself ends.

Each life is a different battlefield. Each person has a different calling to fight in a different set of evils and trials. Some fight in daylight, in pitched battles with clearly drawn lines, victories, and losses. Others fight in black alleyways, bringing light into dark places. Still others are called into a spiritual Forlorn Hope. They are called to lives of pain, suffering, confusion, wounds, and seeming defeat. I do not think that I am being melodramatic when I claim to be part of that group.

Let me tell you a little about myself and why I'm writing this book at all.

In late October of 2011, I was a passenger in a car accident. That accident caused severe brain damage and led to a life that I would never have imagined living. As of the time I write this, I live in a constant state of pain due to a headache of immense magnitude that never leaves. I have nightmares every time I close my eyes to sleep, and I often doubt the world around me when I wake. I have precious little energy from day to day and it often takes herculean effort just to accomplish simple, household tasks. I have slipped into psychotic episodes, hallucinations, delusions, and compulsive obsessions that have occasionally even robbed me of my free-will.

However, the most dramatic aspect of my condition is the anterograde amnesia, a medical condition that limits my memory, post-accident, to roughly six hours or so (though, with time and therapy, I have brought it up to nearly 14 hours as of November 2015 — see epilogue for notes on my recovery as of the publication of this book, which is over a year since the writing of the rough draft). My memories last for a certain time and then fade out into nothingness, leaving me stranded on the far side of an ever-widening gap between my present and my past. I cannot remember any of the details of life between the accident and the writing of this book. My life is governed and limited by a notebook that I use to keep track of everything that happens — at least a single page's worth of it at a time.

Because of my brain damage, I had to drop out of a prestigious university and my United States Marine Corps scholarship and future commission were revoked. Everything that I had trained for in my life was suddenly gone — and I am never getting it back.

I have even doubted aspects of my own humanity because, throughout all of this, I feel nothing. I have been robbed of all emotional responses to the stimuli of life. I do not get angry, sad, happy, or hopeful. And my limits are not only emotional. The worst of it is this: I cannot connect with God like I used to. I do not feel the pleasure of God when I do good nor his sorrow when I do evil. I feel no refreshing grace in times of prayer (alone or communal). When I drink in the Word, I am not refreshed in a way I can actively experience. This lack of feeling, and many of the despicable things I have done while psychotic and obsessive, have led me to even have doubts about my salvation. The Bible doesn't say much about brain damage.

However, while I doubt myself, my place, and even the world around me at any given moment, there are some things I know about God and I know that they have not changed because He does not change.

This book has been inspired by my circumstances and I hope that it will accomplish three things for you, my readers.

Primarily, I hope that my story will call out to others who fight alongside me in The Forlorn Hope. Though smoke and darkness divide us, we fight the same fight. You do not fight utterly alone. In this book, I will share truths that have helped me in my own fight and which I hope will help you as well.

Second, I hope to help those who may not be called to fight in the same way as I am, the "Caregivers", to understand a bit more about the battle. These Caregivers are any and all who want to help, serve, and encourage those who suffer. You are the church members, the small group leaders, the friends, and the family of those of us in The Forlorn Hope. We who fight in The Forlorn Hope are not better or worse people for it. We are still sinners saved by grace and adopted by God just like everyone who Christ died for — but our lives and battles are going to look very different from most and may be difficult to relate to. Nearly all chapters will have a few words directed toward you.

Last, I want to remind every one of my readers of some of the truths about God that we all need to keep in mind for our daily struggles. These truths may not always be directly stated and sometimes may only be alluded to, but they are there.

The format of this book is a little unusual. Each chapter is begun with a poem that I wrote about a particular truth or circumstance and is then continued through a page or two of prose. Why poetry? Well, for two reasons. First, because I'm better at writing poetry than I am at most other forms of writing and so I had started this book out as a collection of poems. Second, because I believe that poetry has the potential to touch the hearts and minds of people in a way that prose can't. The rhythms, rhyme, and other poetic tools aren't just there to be beautiful, they actually have an impact on the reader (or listener — they sound best when read aloud). Now, before you get worried that I wrote a great deal of esoteric, inaccessible poetry and shoehorned it into a book on suffering, I want to assure you that that is not what I have done at all. The poetry you will read in this book is simple, clear, and mostly concise. It is designed to put truth into a package that doesn't just affect the mind, but the heart as well, and is open to everyone to understand.

I hope it helps.

One last note before you begin. I have arranged the chapters in the order that I thought would be most impactful. Since they have been written over a long time, there might be references to my age or to the timeline of my progression of that don't make chronological sense. My recommendation is that, as you read, you ignore the chronology and simply focus on the ideas and truths being presented. Time is a funny thing — especially for me — but the truths themselves are (I hope) timeless. As you read each chapter, feel free to let it stand alone without having to depend on context of the rest.

The Forlorn Hope

I fight because I choose to fight.
I choose because I was chosen.
The One who chose commands my might
though I be battered and broken.

I bend and mold my shattered arm
'till it becomes a bloody wing.
But I'll not fly away from harm.
No, fighting is the only thing
that's left to me. No joys of peace.
I will not live to see war cease
but I will choose to fight until
my body's slain and I lay still.

So tempt me not and say that I
will ever see the sun again.
Do not entice me with a lie
of grassy fields and green-lit glen.

The battle I must fight is deep
below the trees and mossy dell.
My arm helps swing the battering ram
that crashes on the gates of hell.
So let the devil quail in fear.
He knows his time is drawing near,
for maybe soon The One who chose
will crack the gate beneath our blows.

So do not weep or fear for me
for this is where I'm called to be —
in darkness, void of any light.
Here am I. I choose to fight.

The Forlorn Hope

Dear Readers,

This was the not the first chapter that I wrote for this book, but I want it to encompass the purpose and drive of the book — or at least the mindset that is inspiring it. I am not a hopeless person, but I do not — I cannot — look around at life and see anything that is not steeped in the pain and battle of a spiritual Forlorn Hope. Even what pleasures I have been given are now coated in pain and suffering. I can see room for improvement, but no end to this experience.

I wrote this poem back when I had intended to simply write a book of poems, so I am having to go back and analyze it again. This is made both easier and harder by the fact that I cannot remember writing it. Amnesia is a funny thing, so I am constantly relearning.

One thing I wish to say right from the beginning is that my life is not hopeless, though the literal translation of the title of this chapter (and book), without context, means just that. Nonetheless, this is not a hopeless chapter. It is not overtly hopeful either, at least not in a temporal way. The hope that I have is the victory that Christ has already won over the enemy, sin, pain, and death, but we will only fully experience that victory when we are called home to Him. There are many who see life the same way.

This specific poem has had an impact on my own life and that only indicates to me that it was God-sent and did not come from any wisdom in myself. I wrote it down in the beginning of the notebook that keeps my life in order. Every morning, I wake up and read the notebook lying next to me. As I relearn all the terrible things that have happened and about all that I have lost since October 2011, I am also reminded of the dreadful glory of the fight I am in. I am reminded of what I am fighting and who I am fighting for. I have read this poem every day for over two years now, and every day it reminds me to continue fighting. It reminds me especially that though God's grace is the strength of my arm, I must choose to swing it. As Paul says in Philippians,

> "Therefore, my beloved, as you have always obeyed, so now, not only as in my presence but much more in my absence, work out your own salvation with fear and trembling, for it is God who works in you, both to will and to work for his good pleasure." (Philippians 2:12-13 ESV)

The bloody wing that carries me into battle and the arm that I use to help swing that heavy ram against the very gates of hell, it is all from God — but it's not something I can simply let happen. They are my hands. This is my life and I must choose to fight even as I have been chosen. I don't fully understand this passage myself. What is God's part and what is mine? I don't know. But I do know that I must fight and that victory will come when Christ returns in power.

I do not know if this idea will have the exact same impact on you as it has on me, but I hope it does. If you too are called to fight in The Forlorn Hope, if these words resonated with you, then perhaps it will encourage you to continue your fight.

To those who are with me in The Forlorn Hope, keep up the fight. If God can work in and through my life to any degree during this time, then I am confident that He can work in and through you as well. I am not comparing our suffering. Each person suffers differently. What I am saying is that Jesus Christ is in your suffering just as He is in mine and He is going to work.

Caregivers, those of you who are not called at this time to fight in The Forlorn Hope, I want you to begin to understand a simple truth from this first chapter: our fight is going to be radically different from yours. The same words and truths are going to apply to us very differently. I'm not saying that we are somehow special or that certain rules in God's law do not apply to us. I'm saying that the principles that are contained in God's Word are going to be worked out in practice differently in the life of a suffering person. The command to rejoice is the same, but the act of rejoicing is going to look different. The call to love applies to us all, but how that love plays out is going to be different because a hurting person's capacity to demonstrate that love is different. The truth stands that God is good, always and forever, but how someone in The Forlorn Hope sees God's goodness is going to be worlds different than someone outside of it.

But isn't it different for everyone? Well, yes. People are unique in their experiences and basic personhood. But those natural differences are exacerbated by suffering. Suffering often takes parts of who someone is and emphasizes them while suppressing other parts.

I will be talking a good deal more about this topic later on in the book. For now, I simply want to leave the Caregivers with the concept that The Forlorn Hope is going to be different from your battles in drastic and profound ways. What you can do with an understanding of these differences, I will touch on later.

He Knows

He knows without you saying anything
about your grief and heavy loss today,
and every day, and what it's like to stay
in pain from dawn to dusk. The God-man, King
of earth and sky and sea and everything
between. He understands your suffering.
He knows

just what it's like to feel the bitter sting
of every friend up and abandoning
then being falsely judged and dragged away
to whipping blocks where soldiers stood to flay
His flesh. This hurt that you're experiencing?
He knows.

He Knows

Dear Readers,

Hebrews 4:15-16 says,
"For we do not have a high priest who is unable to sympathize with our weaknesses, but one who in every respect has been tempted as we are, yet without sin. Let us then with confidence draw near to the throne of grace, that we may receive mercy and find grace to help in time of need." (ESV)

C hrist is the perfect companion to a suffering soul. *He knows* everything that you are going through — and not just as an observer, but as someone who has gone through suffering just like yours. He's not merely someone cautiously approaching you to deliver a timid platitude, nor is he an oaf who throws out a wild or hurtful guess at what you need to hear. He knows exactly what to say to help you endure.

Now, what Christ communicates to you in your suffering may not be what you think you need to hear. It may not *feel* particularly comforting, though it *will* be what you really do need to hear. And because He knows exactly what to say to you, you ought to always listen to Him. Shutting out the words of your Savior in times of pain is only going to make things worse.

How do you know what He's trying to say? The princi- ples for listening to the voice of God amidst suffering are the same as in times of peace: quiet your heart and go to God and his Word in prayer. James 5:13 says "Is anyone among you suffering? Let him pray," (ESV). The 'quieting your heart' bit is going to be rough when suffering, I know. Sometimes when your heart is in agony, you aren't able to do much besides feel pain. I am not recommending long, eloquent, puritanical prayers. I am saying that if you are going to look for clarity and comfort and peace, the one place that those might be found is in the presence of God. But in The Forlorn Hope, just as in times of peace, you are not guaranteed an immediate answer. God might remain quiet as His message waits for the right time to reach you. Don't despair when you don't hear it right away. Keep listening.

Another way that we often hear from God is rather more difficult to receive in The Forlorn Hope. And that is when God speaks through other people into our lives. It's easy to be isolated by pain (pain is an isolating thing) and often, others' attempts to help are mixed with mistakes which can cause even more pain. But while you aren't called to take someone else's words as gospel, when you hear the gospel in their words, you ought to grab on to it. For those of you in The Forlorn Hope with me, please do not entirely shut out those around you. Your Savior knows what you feel and He knows what you need and He will send you the people that are going to be best for you — even if you do not understand His selection. You cannot afford to shut out any avenues of grace in this battle. Though, I would caution you that not every person will always be an avenue of grace. You have to be discerning about who is hurting more than helping. That said, not everyone who errs is someone to avoid. If you shut everyone out, you may have thrown the baby out with the bathwater.

A word to the Caregivers: you are not the perfect com-forter and never will be. Christ is. The best thing that you can do for someone in The Forlorn Hope is to point them, gently and lovingly, to God. This doesn't mean, however, that you shouldn't also try to care for them directly through other words and actions. As you learn their needs, you can try some direct comforting. But the best human comforters know to point someone to the best Comforter.

We Know a Little

We know a little what it's like to cry
in our own personal Gethsemane.
And no, our sweat's not blood like His but we
are weeping for a cup we must drink dry.
And no, our suffering won't justify
a soul. But what He did for you and me?
We know a little

about what it is like to say goodbye
to all we treasured, then have friends deny
their promises to us and run off free
while we are crushed. By this tragedy
of smaller deaths that we are called to die
we know a little.

We Know a Little

Dear Readers,

This chapter is a close companion to the previous one. These two truths go together. You see, shared suffering forms a two-way street for us and our Savior. It is true that Christ knows every ounce of our suffering personally. It is also true that all who suffer know a little about what it was like for Christ to suffer and die for us. 2 Corinthians 1:5 says "For as we share abundantly in Christ's sufferings, so through Christ we share abundantly in comfort too." That comfort is the truth of the gospel and the promises of our heavenly Father. The closer we are to Christ in his suffering, the closer we are to the comfort of His truth and love.

It may not feel like it, but this pain is, in some ways, a privilege. Those of us set in The Forlorn Hope are given a unique perspective on the work of God when we share in the sufferings of Christ. In fact, this broken world that we live in is the only place that offers us this unique opportunity "into which angels long to look" (1 Peter 1:12 ESV). Once we get to heaven, our time of sharing in the sufferings of Christ will be finished, as will our suffering. Thank God!

We ought to learn as much as we can here while we can. This is something I've tried to live out and God has been faithful to teach me. I know a lot more than I used to (though still only a miniscule fraction) of what He went through for me. And I love Him all the more for it (in my own passion-less way). Knowing excruciating physical pain has taught me to better appreciate the crucifixion. Knowing the aban-donment of close friends taught me a bit of what it was like for Jesus to be left alone when he was arrested. Having my experience of God cut off in this small way has taught me the barest sliver of what Christ must have gone through when the Father turned his back. He went through all that for me to a degree that I cannot even imagine — and because of my own sufferings, I can imagine a lot. And by knowing more of what Christ's love led him through for me, it becomes that much more essential that I show His love to others. "By this we know love, that he laid down his life for us, and we ought to lay down our lives for the brothers." 1 John 3:16 (ESV).

To those who are suffering, I gently urge you not to treat your suffering as a gateway only to evil but as a chance to peek through a window on the journey of Christ to the cross. This perspective will grow your love for Christ and for those around you. You are being given an excruciating gift. Don't turn it aside because of the pain. I am not suggesting to you that you should be happy about your pain, but to see that there is more to it than evil. There is beauty to be understood about The One who suffered for you, and there is love that will overflow when you do.

Caregivers, I do not recommend sharing the truth that you can know more about God through suffering as com-fort unless you know this through your own experience. It is something that may be received best from someone else intimately acquainted with pain. It is difficult for many of us in The Forlorn Hope to accept explanations of the benefits of pain from someone who hasn't been there themselves. That isn't to say that you should never try to encourage with this truth. There are very few hard and fast rules for caring for someone in suffering. I can only make recommendations to you in this book, and my recommendation for applying this truth directly is to approach it cautiously if at all.

Now, there is certainly a way you can help indirectly. You can learn from those who are in The Forlorn Hope. They are being given a chance to understand Jesus's work in a unique way. Let them teach you through their words and actions so that you might be able to understand a bit more as well. By allowing them to teach you, you will be reinforcing this understanding in their own mind and soul. They say that the best way to learn is to teach, and there's truth to that. So, try to learn. It is a way for you to grow and to help.

Old Before My Time

There's nothing ages quite like pain does
or slows the time that slips on by.
A moment seems a dozen moments.
A year's a decade in the eye
of someone hurting. Can you see them?
Bowed down beneath the weight of just
another day? The backs that once were
so strong and straight are bent. They rust
like swingsets left out in the weather.
The legs that strode up mountainsides
now creak and pop like old ship's timbers
on ever changing ocean tides.

I once was young and dreamed like young men
of glory and adventure too.
I built my life up into something
that someday I'd be proud of. Who
could guess that fearful strife was inbound
or that I'd live to see the day
when I would leave the war to other
eager boys to go and play?
Now I do not seek future glory
I do not strive for greatness. No,
my dreams are of release from all this —
an end to time that goes so slow.

Old Before My Time

Dear Readers,

As I write these words, I feel old. As of this moment, I am only 23 years old (soon to be 24). That's not so old, is it? It can be. The first line of the poem is very true — pain ages people. Look in the eyes of a child who grew up in a war-ravaged country where suffering is constant and life is hard. He may have some fun in a lighthearted moment, but he grew up the day he watched his parents gunned down by the local warlord's soldiers. Now, I am not comparing my pain to a child from a third-world country. I am simply offering an undeniable example of a principle that applies to some extent to all who suffer. For those of us called to The Forlorn Hope, pain is an everyday thing, a constant companion that piles years onto shoulders that might have once been young.

I have many pains — much like the elderly. My head splits as though someone is attacking it with an axe. My lower back aches from scar tissue leftover from a botched spinal tap in the winter of 2012. My right knee has been battered just by walking on it, due to the accident leaving the right side of my body weakened. I often walk with a cane to support myself so I don't keel over suddenly (author's note: by 2014 God in His kindness has mostly healed my knee through therapy, though it is still not completely whole). Like someone with Alzheimer's, I can't remember what I ate for breakfast this morning. Also, like the elderly, I am losing touch with the world. I cannot remember the latest updates in technology or who is dating or married to whom (my own brother is getting married soon as of the writing of this poem). As a younger man, this is perhaps unique to my own particular brand of suffering, but I think that it may also apply to others as well. Suffering is isolating, and in isolation you often lose touch. But I am reassured by a truth that doesn't change: truth doesn't change. The world around me may change, but Christ remains Lord. Hebrews 13:8 (ESV) says, "Jesus Christ is the same yesterday and today and forever." I may age and grow infirm more rapidly than most, but God remains good. I may not be able to physically remember one moment of God's faithfulness in the recent years of my life, but I *know* that He is faithful. I know Him, and in knowing Him, I can rest assured that I will age in His good time and reach my rest when He calls me to it (though I often pray that it is soon).

To those who suffer, remember that as you age (perhaps more quickly than others), there is one who does not age; one who remains the same from age to age. Isaiah 46:4 says, "...even to your old age I am he, and to gray hairs I will carry you. I have made, and I will bear; I will carry and will save." Your Heavenly Father will be no different tomorrow even if you are. He doesn't forget His promise, even if you do.

Caregivers, I am going to reiterate and expand on the point I made in the first chapter. Remember that those who are in The Forlorn Hope are not going to see the world the same way that you do. Even if they are young, they might not be able to pull long nights to spend time with a friend. They might not have the energy to be a part of large groups of people. They might not be able to keep focused or have the mental/emotional fortitude to hold a decent conversation. They may just be weighed down with the enormity of their suffering. When this is the case, you *must* recognize that they are limited. However, my counsel to you is to try to treat them as an equal but without patronizing them. You must not push them too far, but you shouldn't treat them like a child either.

This is sometimes a hard balance to find, and I know that I am asking a lot for the sake of those of us in The Forlorn Hope. But caring for someone — that deep, selfless, sacrifice of showing Christ's love to someone in immense pain — takes work. I pray that God gives you the grace to be able to find this balance.

Suffering of Mystery

Sometimes the cause of our hurting is clear
and sometimes it's not. God grabbing our ear
and correcting our sin hurts. And the dear
friends who stab our backs? That hurts. Every year
those we love take another step towards death
and their final breath provokes a tear.

But there's one other kind that I want you
to know. And you can't know it through and through
unless you've been there, but I want you to
know it exists. So before you pursue
someone hurting, please remember this truth:
there's suffering of mystery too.

Think back to Job's three friends who came to see
him in his pain. They looked for normalcy
and ways to explain the discrepancy
of Job's goodness and his adversity.
Then God *Himself* rebuked them for the words
He overheard from their audacity.

The ways of God are high — so very high!
His simplest reasons alone defy
explanation. He'll rarely clarify
The Forlorn Hope to us. So when you try
to say "oh this is how it works, I know,"
you throw darts but with tightly shut eyes.

Sometimes there's reasons that only God knows
of. It's not always sin or human foes
or loss. And God does not always disclose
the real reason. So before you oppose
someone on the assumption of their sin,
remember, in love: never suppose.

Suffering of Mystery

Dear Readers,

This is one of several poems included in this book that were inspired by Tim Keller's book 'Walking with God through Pain and Suffering.' I've learned a lot from that book over the months I have read and re-read it. Some of the truths have even sunk into my subconscious mind after enough repetition, though I can't always remember where I learned them. In his book, Keller wrote a chapter titled 'The Varieties of Suffering'. It helped me put specific terms to an idea that I had been putting around the edges of: not all suffering is the same. In 'The Varieties of Suffering', Keller lays out several different kinds of suffering.[1]

There is the suffering we cause ourselves by our own sin (e.g. Jonah). There is the suffering of betrayal (e.g. Paul's betrayal by the Jews). There is the suffering of loss that everyone experiences when people and things they love are taken away from them (e.g. Mary, Martha, and Lazarus). And then there is the suffering of mystery. Keller uses two perfect examples in Job and Sons of Korah (in Psalm 44) to explain this. Sometimes there is suffering with causes and reasons known only to God. Perhaps the suffering has been allowed for purposes that are too high for us to understand. Or maybe part of the experience that God desires for us involves knowing nothing of why we suffer. For whatever reason, there are times when we suffer for causes that no human being can fathom, and this is most often where people find themselves in The Forlorn Hope.

Before I specifically address those suffering, I want to drive a point home to the Caregivers. You *must* understand the truth that not all suffering is brought about by someone's sin. Granted, it is because we live in a sinful, broken world that suffering even exists, but someone in pain might not be suffering because of their own sin. God Himself bragged of Job's righteousness and then put him through more suffering than nearly any person in history save Christ Himself.

So, I beg you, do not ever — ever — assume that someone is suffering because of his or her own sin. Please do not try to help someone in The Forlorn Hope by searching for sin first, assuming it to be the root of the problem. That is a horrifyingly effective way to add weight to the burden of someone already suffering greatly. Go, read through Job. See what God says to Job's three friends after they tried to rationalize Job's suffering by accusing him of sin. Those words are for you who do the same, blaming someone for their trials as if those trials are obviously their own fault. I will talk more in the next chapter about how to approach someone who is in suffering and also in sin.

To those who are suffering, I want you also to be aware of this truth, but you must be careful with it as well. On one hand, you should never dismiss the possibility that your suffering might be the suffering of mystery. For those of you truly in The Forlorn Hope, do not let the ignorance of those around you (or your own fears) convince you that you must be doing something wrong for you to have to suffer like this. That is a lie. You do not need to beat yourself up or consider it your own doing. That will only add condemnation to your suffering and that will only sink you lower.

On the other hand, not all suffering is solely the mysterious sort. Do not always assume that your suffering is never your own doing. The different sufferings are not mutually exclusive. You can be experiencing several or perhaps even all of them together. Don't sink into a self-pitying, victim mindset every time something hurts. I know that this is sometimes a hard distinction to make. It's not a horrible idea to check your own heart for sin when some kinds of suffering visit you — but don't insist to yourself that sin *must* be there if you are suffering, no matter what anyone says. Sometimes even the best intentioned people can mistake The Forlorn Hope for a sin-issue. Please forgive them.

This is a tricky subject to address, I'm aware. I hope I have helped you to understand a bit more about the nature of suffering. I will pray that God gives you wisdom to distinguish between the different kind of suffering so that you can walk through them (or help someone else walk through them) as best you can.

Till Your Own Heart's Been Broken

Should physicists give lectures in history
or historians teach engineers?
Should arm-chair reporters judge war-hardened soldiers?
Should you rebuke people in tears?

And are you a good enough person,
with humility, wisdom, and care
to tell me the difference between unrepentance
and suffering when they're *both* there?

Until your own heart has been broken
and you have been wounded in battle
you have little right to speak into their fight
or give yourself leave to prattle.

So if you see someone bereaved and in sin
before you go and jump right in,
ask yourself
"Have I the right
to speak?"

Till Your Own Heart's Been Broken

Dear Readers,

Few authors have affected my life and faith like C.S. Lewis. I have read nearly everything he has written and each word has spoken to my soul. This chapter was inspired by a passage from Lewis' work 'The Great Divorce'. In that book, Lewis (the first-person narrator of the book) overhears a conversation between a redeemed spirit in Heaven and a damned spirit from Hell who has been given the opportunity to stay in Heaven, if she will release her selfish hold on her son, who died while she was still living and is already far off into the mountains of glory. She demands that her son be brought to her and in the end states that she would rather have her son with her in Hell to be hers alone than to join him in Heaven and have him belong to God. Of course, she has no power to drag her boy to Hell, so that is not the outcome. The book leaves off that conversation before it reaches its end, but it gives a good setting for the next bit of dialogue between Lewis and his guide, George MacDonald.

Addressing the fact that the woman is clearly in the wrong but is also in deep suffering, Lewis asks, "But could one dare — could one have the face — could one go to a bereaved mother, in her misery — when one's not bereaved oneself?" To which MacDonald replies with words that I will never forget, "No, no, son. That's no office of yours. You're not a good enough man for that. When your own heart's been broken, it will be time for you to think of talking." [2] Now, I want to approach this topic somewhat delicately but also firmly. This is related to but not a direct continuation of the last chapter. This time I am assuming that the person in suffering *is* in sin. This is addressing the idea that someone in The Forlorn Hope is not suffering well or that they have tried seeking comfort and satisfaction from some source other than God and His gifts.

This is a very tricky situation for everyone. How can you tell what is sin and must be cut out and what is simply a result of someone suffering — something they can't help? It can be a difficult distinction to make. So, here is my advice to the Caregivers: stop and think VERY carefully before you say anything. Be aware that sometimes you will not be in a position where you ought to speak into someone's life— even about their sin. Are you able to tell the difference between self-pity and depression? Are you able to tell the difference between grief and bitterness? Are you able to tell the difference between laziness and fatigue? Can you tell me what is bereavement and what is selfishness in the heart of a mother grieving her lost child? Few people are able to discern these, and those who can are either phenomenally good human beings or (more likely) have suffered greatly themselves.

So, there are two calls I want to send out with this poem. First, to the Caregivers, I want you to generally hold back from *solely* correcting the sin of someone in suffering. There are a few exceptions to this, but they must be approached cautiously. It may be acceptable to bring up the sin of someone in suffering if there is no one else to do it. If they are unrepentantly stuck in sin and no one is saying anything, it *might* be your duty to speak up, but in doing so, remain mindful of their suffering. Another exception would be if the person in suffering has specifically asked you to speak to their sin. You obviously then have permission to do so–but don't forget that they are in pain. There isn't a formula that I can give you for the correct method of rebuke for someone in The Forlorn Hope. Though I would ask that you remain patient, gracious, and mindful of the forgiveness that God has extended to you and to the suffering sinner that you are approaching. Those who have effectively corrected me since my accident have done so with a love that expressed sorrow over my sin, not anger or judgement. They have graciously reminded me not only of my duty, but of the God who loves and claims me as His own. They have made me aware that there is not only failing on my part, but forgiveness and grace to change from my Maker. And, perhaps most importantly, those dear friends did not stop meeting my needs even while they saw sin in my life. Please, if you are going to rebuke someone in The Forlorn Hope, remember these principles: love, forgiveness, and the meeting of needs.

Finally, if you are in a position of church leadership, I believe that you have a responsibility to address someone's sin. Here, I'm going to be bold (as a layman) and address any pastors or clergy who may be reading this book. You must not forget that someone is made up of more than their sins. It is your job as leaders and elders in the church to address it at times, yes, but it is also your job to care for those in suffering as sufferers, not just sinners. Do not define someone by their sins alone. If all you do is address the sin of someone hurting without addressing their pain, they are going to think that you are seeing only sin in them. This does far more harm than help, especially if coming from church leadership. It may end up driving someone hurting and in sin away from the church — which is right where they need to be. The application of this principle is going to differ with each person and situation, but it is not impossible to find the right mix if you keep the principle in mind.

To those in The Forlorn Hope, I want you to take up a heavy responsibility. I know that I am asking much of you, but I believe that this is part of the calling on those of us who suffer. We must band together as much as possible and encourage one another towards righteousness, correcting and rebuking if need be. We who fight in this smoke and confusion know better than most what is sin and what is pain. We live there. It is our world. If you are honest with yourself, you know that you need correction and encouragement too– we all do. So, in love and in humility and in the knowledge that you have gained through your own suffering, help spur others on towards righteousness and away from sin. That's one of the reasons I'm writing this book.

Promised

Send rest, oh Lord,
if just for a moment.
I'm so very weary on this road.

Where is the easy yoke?
Where is the light burden?
You promised rest to those who came
weary and heavy laden.
Well, here I am.
Where are You?

You promised strength
to those who wait —
"Like eagles," You said.
How long must I wait for You?

I *know* you!
At least, I know You well enough
to know You never break a promise.

You promised...

Perhaps I'm like the thief who was crucified by your side
who had to suffer the agonies of his own cross
before joining You in paradise.

So I guess I'll carry my cross
and hang upon it, too, if that's what you call for
and wait as long as need be
for You to fulfill
Your promise.

Promised

Dear Readers,

I'm not entirely sure what to say in addition to this poem. It lays out my questions rather plainly. Am I questioning God's promises? Not really. I'm asking Him questions (because I don't know and I know He does), but I'm not questioning who He is. I know that He is faithful and I know that He is good, wise, and powerful, and I trust that He will keep His Word. I just don't know how.

I'm not certain that I will ever rest again in this world or know a peaceful mind. Perhaps I'll have to wait until heaven to experience the fulfillment of some of His promises, or perhaps I am already experiencing their fulfillment in some way that I'm not aware of. Perhaps I'm simply too confused and blinded by pain and sin to know what God is doing in me and for me. What I will do is keep delving into His word and lifting my voice in prayer, drawing as close to Christ as I can. If there is peace or understanding, I'll find it in the presence of Christ. And if there is none, I will try to be content to wait to know and understand. I know that I will someday.

This chapter is really intended to communicate a bit of my suffering to you — or at least my thoughts in the midst of it. I know what it is like to call out with David in Psalm 22:1, "My God, my God, why have you forsaken me?" I know the agony and the utter lack of knowing why. No, I don't believe that God has completely forsaken me, and I believe that He has not forsaken you either, but He has withdrawn many of His temporal blessings. I will never know fully why until heaven. I don't mean this chapter to exacerbate your despair — only to let you know that I understand what it is to question the purpose of God's actions. I am not writing this book in ignorance of what it is like to be overwhelmed by questions of "why?" and "how long?"

Caregivers, you must simply know that sometimes we who suffer are in this place of questioning, and that it is *not* a place of sin. This is an example of the principle that I talked about in the chapter, 'Suffering of Mystery'. This is one area where crying out in response to all the suffering that God seems to be orchestrating is not a wrongdoing. When someone cries out in pain, do you reprimand them? No, and I do not think it is your place to do so here, either. You are free to remind them of the person of God (like Elihu to Job), but do not rebuke someone who cries out in the darkness because they cannot see the light. God will reveal all things in time–but it is not wrong to cry out in bewilderment when He has not yet revealed anything.

In his book, 'Walking With God Through Pain and Suffering', Tim Keller talks about suffering as both just and unjust, a result of a broken world but still under the sovereignty of God. He says, "because suffering is both just and unjust, we can cry out and pour out our grief, yet without the toxic additive of bitterness." [3] That is not to say that we in The Forlorn Hope are immune from bitterness, or even permitted bitterness, but it does mean that we are able to weep, mourn, and groan without it necessarily being tied into bitterness. If you see someone stuck in bitterness, it might be worth speaking up about it (though I would recommend that you approach that situation in the way I explained in the last chapter) — but be mindful that not all wailing is the result of someone's sin.

Let Us Be Good

Let us be good to one another now
for often those around us cannot know
the depth of wounds that lay a body low,
or how much pain our Father will allow.

And to my siblings trudging through the slough,
we'll trudge together though the way is slow.
Let us be good to one another now
for often those around us cannot know.

And while our wounds and bogs are different. How
we thirst for comfort is the same. And though
our battles don't compare each blow for blow,
a knowing kindness helps the most somehow.
Let us be good to one another now.

Let us be Good

My Dear Readers,

This idea is another of mine that has been inspired by the works of C.S. Lewis. Perhaps one of the most moving moments in all The Chronicles of Narnia is in the Magician's Nephew when Digory, despite being charged with the marring of a good new world, begs the Great Lion Aslan for some magic to help his dying mother. When he looks up into Aslan's face, he sees tears there. "My son, my son," said Aslan "I know. Grief is great. Only you and I in this land know that yet. Let us be good to one another."

When I first heard those words, read to me by my parents, I was far too young to understand them. But coming back to them years later, I find them to be as profound as words can be. We who have suffered — especially those who have suffered greatly — ought to be good to one another. The kindness of someone who doesn't know what it means to hurt the way we have is not to be scoffed at, but at the same time, there is no substitute for kindness that knows (at least a bit) what it is like to be undone.

Many things can keep us from being good to one another. Sometimes, we are too caught up in our own suffering to notice the wounds of others. It is no sin to be overwhelmed by suffering at times — but when we can, we ought to look around to see what goodness we can do. Other times, we do see the suffering of others and we compare it to our own. Humans are creatures of competition. When we compare, we will often rate another person's suffering higher or lower than our own. We might see them as having suffered worse than ourselves and say "What can I say to that?" or we might see them as having less pain than us and say "Why should I be good to them? Aren't I hurting worse?" Neither of these are helpful frames of mind for ourselves or for others. Comparison is the enemy of kindness.

The rule is, "be good." And in fact, that rule applies to everyone, so comparison doesn't enter into it at all, really. But you should try to be discerning. If you are in The Forlorn Hope (or have been in it) and you see someone living in it now and you can in humble truthfulness say to them, "I know — let us be good to one another," then I believe that you ought to. When someone can truly say, "I understand," and then follows that up with "let's be good to one another" — it will be a blessing beyond words to someone suffering.

What does it mean to be good to one another? I'm afraid I can't tell you. There are many, many ways to do this well and many, many ways to do this poorly. I can't tell you exactly what to say or do. There is no formula. You who have suffered will simply have to make an educated guess based on your own experience and understanding of truth. It's what I do myself — in some ways that's what I'm doing with this book.

To the Caregivers out there: making the statement "I know" is not something you can fully do unless you have been in The Forlorn Hope yourself. I'm not trying to drive you away — but if you say this to someone who doesn't believe that you understand, you may drive *them* away. The pretense of knowledge in the midst of ignorance is one of the surest ways to alienate someone truly suffering. But you can always be good to someone. There is no limit to that. You do not have to know exactly how someone is hurting to be kind, gracious, and helpful. I'll explain a little bit more about this in the next chapter.

The Least of These

We're different but the same,
we who suffer.
We need the same things
but in different ways,
the same encouragement
but with different words,
the same people
with a different dynamic,
the same truth
with a different perspective,
the same God
with a different appreciation
for His love.

And yes, we know it's hard
to stick it through
and learn the differences we have.
It's uncomfortable to spend your time
with someone hurting.
It takes unthinkable patience
to stay and learn the ins and outs
of what we need
and who we are.

Despite all of that,
I'm asking you to stay.
There are countless
sufferers around you
who need a friend.
We are the least of these,
my brothers.

The Least of These

Dear Readers,

This chapter, as you can probably tell, is geared more towards those outside The Forlorn Hope, The Caregivers, than those inside it. It is, I hope, a passionately-worded plea for help aimed at those who are not suffering in The Forlorn Hope. Those of us who are suffering need friends to help us stay afloat. We need compassion and fellowship to build up our spirits for the battles we must face on a daily basis.

How can you help? It's both easy and arduous, simple yet devilishly complex.

A hurting person has the same primary needs (in principle) as someone who is not hurting. That is, they need to be built up, encouraged, and pointed back to their Maker through both words and actions. This should be the core of any Christian friendship.

But what does that look like? That's where it gets complex. You see, the specific needs are vastly different for each and every suffering person. There's no formula to plug in for what to do or what to say. There is, however, a secret to figuring out what a suffering person needs, though it may jar you with its simplicity and perhaps its obviousness. Here it is: get to know them.

Just get to know them. Again, this is simple in principle, but hard to execute. You get to know someone in The Forlorn Hope the same way as you get to know anyone. You spend time with them. You *listen* much more than you speak at first. Ask thoughtful questions, and from their answers, build an idea of who they are. Learn about their thoughts and feelings. Discover their perspective on God. Try and discern their motivations — what makes them tick. When you have done this, try to meet the needs of theirs that you are equipped to meet. As you grow closer to the person, you will begin to uncover both who they are in suffering (this may be very different from who they are or were outside of suffering) and what they need in their place of suffering.

As I said in the introductory poem, I know that this is hard. It takes patience with our weakness and agony, forgiveness for our faults and lashing out, understanding that we do not always understand ourselves, and a willingness to leave comfort behind to help someone. I think this last part may be the hardest in this present day and age, particularly in the prosperous West. We love, crave, and even worship comfort — and the Church is not immune to this. In general, American Christendom is not particularly good at caring for people in deep suffering, and I think our idolization of comfort is one of the main reasons why. It's *un*comfortable to get close to someone in suffering. It causes you to wrestle with tough questions about the goodness and plan of God. You may even begin to feel some of the pain of seeing someone you care about in suffering. But I beg you to try anyway.

So, this is my request, if you aren't doing this already: find someone suffering and befriend them. Get to know them. Take whatever discomfort and pain come. Discover how best to serve them, and then do it. There are many unmet needs among those of us who are hurting. Remember what Jesus himself said in Matthew 25:40, "Truly, I say to you, as you did it to one of the least of these my brothers, you did it to me."

To those in The Forlorn Hope, I have a few things to say to you as well. To you, my suffering brothers and sisters, I say that there is no shame in asking for help. There is no sin in asking those around you to try to understand and to aid you in your struggle. When they do offer to help, please accept it whenever you can. I am calling out to the Caregivers to help, but there is little they can do if you reject them. Their help is not going to be perfect, especially not at first, but in the long run, it is going to do some good. Though we are sometimes indeed forced to be alone, we were ultimately meant to live and suffer in community. Your community is not going to be perfect, but I beg you not to shut them out entirely. God can work wonders even through the grossly imperfect.

A Mother's Tears

Drop after drop is lost in a forest of freckles on a weathered face
escaping from beautiful crow-footed eyes as if they were
chased by a savage beast.
They pause only where the cheek is creased to sparkle then go
along the way where all tears flow: to the kitchen tabletop
where they stop and disembark
in a scratch mark left by little hands that used to be my own.
I'd thrown a cookie cooling-rack when I was mad.
I remember feeling so bad to see her cry then —
but that was back when I also could cry.
It was barely a second before my own little eyes welled up
with water.
I never fought her that I didn't cry later on.
But it's all gone now.
I often wonder how the world can carry on in this way.
Nothing can seem to stay for good for long.
Right becomes wrong and little fingers become meaty
grabbers.
Dutiful children become backstabbers and leave their
mothers crying
in the kitchen, dying for a chance to bring them back
to the right track. But tears can only affect those who can
cry themselves.
There, underneath the shelves of dried food
she nearly comes unglued right in front of me
and I, as I see her pain, all I do is watch her weep.
I am an inhuman heap of skin and bone
with her in the room but leaving her alone.

A Mother's Tears

My Dear Readers,

I wrote this poem right after having a conversation with my mother in which we discussed some of the darker places that my broken mind had taken me. I had fallen into deep sin and only partially because of my mental instability. This is a conversation that no one ever wants to have with their mother. She was the one who had taught me right from wrong along with my first words. She changed my diapers and taught me to sing hymns as I was learning basic addition. It was heartbreaking for her.

But for me? I felt nothing. At this point in my life, my condition still rejected any emotional connections or feelings at all. I was firmly convinced that this somehow made me less human. I couldn't feel shame over my actions, and worse, I couldn't feel the powerful regret over causing my mother pain. I asked myself, "How can God love me when I can do such things with no feelings of remorse and dry eyes?"

I had to lean back on what I knew: whatever I was, my Father didn't change. He *is* Love, and since on the cross His Son bore the wrath meant for me, there can be nothing but love for me now. "There is therefore now no condemnation for those who are in Christ Jesus" (Romans 8:1). In Lamentations, a book full of the pain and sin of a people, the author writes, "The steadfast love of the Lord never ceases" (Lamentations 3:22). Somehow in the midst of my pain, sin, and even doubts about my humanity, there was still love for me. There had once been a time in my life when I knew in my mind and my spirit that I was loved by God. And I know that that love never leaves. So, by simple logic, if God's love never ceases, and I once had that love, then I must still have it. It is counterintuitive to us at times, but true.

No matter what you have lost, no matter how far you have fallen, no matter how broken you are, no matter what thoughts you may have about your own humanity — *you are still loved*! You are the object of the holy, eternal, limitless, fiery, overwhelming, terrifying love of God. You may not feel it, but you are loved like that. No matter how much you hurt, no matter who you have hurt, you are loved. I hope that there is someone out there in this world who loves you too — but even if there is not, there is One who loves better than any other could. You might not know who or what you are — I know how that hurts — but you are someone loved by God. That means more about you than anything else ever could.

And while I know it may mean little to you, I want you to know that I love you. I cannot feel the emotions of affection but I can look out through the distance to imagine where you are in your own Forlorn Hope and I can pass on to you the unconditional love that God has given me. I love you, my Dear Readers, and I write these words and every word in this book out of that love. I hope it shows.

Caregivers, you will be hurt by those who suffer. It is inevitable. We are broken people — more broken than most. We will lash out. We will break codes. We will overindulge. We will blaspheme. We will be cruel. We may even break your heart. I am not excusing it. It is wrong and I wish we didn't do these things. On behalf of all of us who suffer in The Forlorn Hope, I ask your forgiveness; I hope that you can find it in your hearts. Please do not give up on us. Remember that you too have been forgiven. I ask that you pass that on to us — as many times as need be.

Rest At Last

I'll rest at last when someday I have died.
"To live is Christ" is all that keeps me tied
to this dark world. But when my time is done,
when all my weary lengths at last are run
and all my bitter tears have then been cried,

I'll sleep, then wake to see the countryside
of God, a place where I won't have to hide
my pain because, once there, there will be none.
I'll rest at last,

and rest from more than pain. There, glorified,
I'll have no more pervasive sin inside.
I'll lay down arms, the battle will be won.
And then, oh then, yes then, I'll see the Son.
And held by nail-scarred hands to wounded side,
I'll rest at last.

Rest at Last

Dear Readers,

This poem is woefully inadequate to serve its purpose. I mean it to inspire hope and longing for that happy country that lies beyond the deep river of death. But how am I to describe Heaven to you? I know nothing of it except that it is a place of peace, beauty, and rest. I do not think that I can find words in my modest vocabulary to tell you how much I desire to see my Savior face to face, to be free of sin and pain, and to rest — finally, truly, fully rest. My body, mind, and soul all ache for that final lying down when I will rise again in a new body, with a pure soul. I want to live in the land where I cannot want anything evil, where I will be free of all earthly weaknesses of mind and physical form. The doubts I had about myself after writing A Mother's Tears will no longer plague me. My brokenness will be made whole.

That day will come. This life is not the end. Our suffering is not the final word.

But though this future has been secured for us, it is not for now. Now, we must follow our Savior's example "who for the joy that was set before him endured the cross" (Hebrews 12:2, ESV). I have my own cross to bear and so do every one of you, Dear Readers. Let us bear our crosses to the end, keeping in mind that to finish the race in Christ means we can finally rest.

I don't have much to say to the Caregivers with this poem, except that this hope in heaven is not limited to those of us who suffer greatly. If you have any discontent in this world, any longing for glory, any eager expectation of the day you will meet your Maker and Savior, it is to be encouraged. This life, no matter the pleasures or pains, is not the end. What comes next is infinitely better.

Pain

Everything is pain
every breath
every thought
my eyes open
my eyes shut

it has a colour
a shape
a taste
the pain is like the air
everywhere
through it i see
everything else

i didn't realize i was starving
i couldn't feel the pangs
in my stomach
for the pain in my head

everything is agony
lifting the fork
typing this poem
trying to come up with words
words are hard.....
i want to use the best words
but they won't come

words are my one things
that I Still have
or so i was thinking

but now
they're not here
they are gone
mostly

I'm not going to ask why
theres no point
God doesn't tell me why

Maybe job was right
it would be better
not to be born

but if i'm going to be like job
then I will be like him
when he said
"blessed be the name of the lord'

God, i know you can read these words
I hope that somehow
I can bring you glory in this
but please
please
if it is in your plan
let it all end.

Pain

My Dear Readers,

This poem is a bit of a mess, I know. I do not apologize. I was a mess when I wrote it. I have left all the spelling, word-choice, and grammar errors in this poem to exemplify that. I do not have a particular truth or message with this poem. It was written during the most painful moments of my life and it is simply me baring my soul and suffering to you.

I am in constant pain — always. It never leaves me. Sometimes it is worse than other times, but it is always severe. I manage it by shoving it behind a door in a corner of my mind and then locking it away. This works most of the time. It allows me to go through everyday life, talk, and think. But sometimes, for one reason or another, it breaks out. During the summer of 2014, I spent nearly a week aching for death. I wasn't actively suicidal (I think–the notes didn't say), but I wanted nothing more than to leave this world and enter the rest of heaven. I do not know exactly what was going through my mind when I wrote this poem. I was not very coherent and the fact that I was able to write this poem down at all is a small miracle.

The pain is mostly under control as of the moment I'm writing this chapter (though there are still spikes of unbridled pain), and I can't remember the pain now — mostly. But it has left a mark. When I look in the mirror and into my own eyes, I can see the scars of it. My conscious mind has forgotten it, but my body can remember. There are echoes of it when something brushes the right side of my head and my whole body jerks and twitches. Pain has changed me.

I am not asking for sympathy in this poem. I am not the sort that thrives on the soothing words of others (though they are not a burden to me most times). I am sharing this to let you know where I have been. Perhaps it is a justification for why I am writing this book at all. I have been there. I have lain like Job in the ash with my robe torn and cried out for God to unmake me. I hope if you are reading this book that you have never been in that position, but I recognize that a distressing number of you have. I only hope that the words of this book can reach you and give you reason and strength to press on even if it is only to croak out a single syllable of praise amidst your cries for the end.

This poem was written long after the previous chapter, but it has not changed the sentiment, only increased it. For those of you who have also cried out for the end in the throes of immeasurable pain, I cannot offer words that will make it go away. I can only hope that my words will help fix your eyes on the end of this world and the glorious beginning of another.

Gray Leaves

It is a rule of nature that
beauty and cruelty often go hand in hand -
the terror of the green depths
the marrow frozen by a white duvet...
and now, for me, the ever-changing masterpiece
of leaves blown by the wind
brings with it chill reminders that
all the warmth of life is gone

In spring I can remember (faintly)
all the many times I smelled the buds of new life.
In summer I can (almost)
re-live the days of boyhood by swimming in a cool lake.
In winter I can don my hat and scarf
and let the icy blast remind me I'm (mostly) alive.
But in autumn... well, autumn was when it happened.
Autumn is where the memories fall short.

I can clearly remember where things become gray.
I can remember the morning of that day:
the sky was a sheet of steel wool
but the cool wind didn't let me feel dull.
I was on my way to worship–my heart was full
but then I slammed that car door shut
and we pulled away.
That's when the leaves, everything, turned gray.

So now despite the vibrant reds, the fall is muted by memory.
And yellows cannot cheer the soul, even when held up in
front of me.
The burning orange reminds me that the fire inside is gone.

And brown leaves underfoot tell me where life was going
all along.

But I can't hate the fall, even now, because that's just how
it goes.
That would be like catching cold and hating your nose.
The year goes on and so will I.
A gray man
walking on gray leaves
under a gray sky.

Gray Leaves

Dear Readers,

I was walking along a road, exploring my way to a new cafe because the diner where I normally sat and wrote was closed on that Sunday morning. As I walked, I was struck by the autumn leaves. Rather, I was struck by how little their vibrant colors affected me. I used to see the shouting array of reds, yellows, and oranges and I would worship. But then the accident happened and now there is no stirring in my soul. There is no impetus to praise. But that day, I realized that even if I cannot worship out of passion, I still must worship. I have to. If I lose that, I will become nothing.

The Westminster Catechism explains in such clear words that the purpose of man is "to glorify God and enjoy Him forever." If we don't glorify God, what are we? And yet if we *do* strive to glorify God, we fulfill our deepest, most solemn, and most beautiful duty.

But we are also called to enjoy God. Here's where I take a little issue with the wording of the Westminster Catechism. You see, there are some of us who aren't capable of enjoying most things. That said, there is a difference between *feeling* joy and rejoicing. One is an experience (outside of our control) and the other is a choice. You may have noticed that while there are many commands to "rejoice" in Scripture, there are none to *feel* joy. The language is not one of emotions. We are commanded to rejoice, but I have found that there are times when God denies us the experience of joy — at least the emotional aspects of it. I think perhaps that joy is a spiritual state rather than an emotional one, though we often confuse the emotional ripples for the spiritual source. I believe that the state of joy is when God brings a soul to a place where the mind attached to it can choose to rejoice, when one gives glory to God and for who He is and what He has done. If you see someone rejoicing, then they are in joy–even if they lack the normal trappings of it and cannot feel it themselves. But this topic is perhaps too great to explore here. For the sake of this book and what I want to communicate here, simply know that feeling joy and rejoicing are two different things.

So, my dear sufferers, do not beat yourself down if you cannot *feel* the joy of the Lord. Do not automatically consider it sin that you do not experience something emotionally. Are you failing to rejoice? If so, you are indeed in sin and someone (perhaps someone who has also suffered) must then consider it their duty to gently rebuke you. You have reason to rejoice in the salvation and promises you have been given. You still serve a good God and One who will gather you to Himself when this life ends. Rejoice — but do not despair if you cannot *feel* the joy of it. It is often in these times of emotional deadness and weakness that our rejoicing brings the most glory to God and does the most to build His kingdom. So, rejoice! Rejoice despite the cold, despite the pain, despite the grayness all around you. Make that terribly hard decision to bring glory to you Savior amidst your pain. I'll talk a bit more about this in the next chapter.

Caregivers, you must understand what I just told those who suffer, but from the outside. When someone in suffering does not feel joyful or does not experience the pleasure of God in something, that does not necessarily mean they are in sin or that something is wrong with them (It might be, but I would refrain from making that judgement unless you have suffered The Forlorn Hope yourself). You ought not to correct them for their experiences, the things that are out of their control. This is another example of the common confusion between suffering and sin. God sometimes denies us certain experiences for reasons that I cannot fathom. So do not rebuke someone for lacking emotional joy. But there may be a way that you can help. My recommendation would be to help lead sufferers to rejoice. Rejoice alongside them and invite them to rejoice with you in the person and truths of God. Beware of the temptation to try to "school" them spiritually. The goal should not be to fix someone, but to worship God with them — He will reveal His truth to them in a deeper way than we can anticipate.

Strike

A soldier lying wounded on the field
cries out to no reply. He will not yield —
not yet — but loathsome monsters hem him in
and stab him with their spears of hate. His shield
hangs limp from broken arm. He
tries to wield his sword against the foe but cannot see
which one to strike among the teeming horde.
His visage writhes in pain as he is gored.
The battle drowns his screams of "why have you
forsaken me? Is it too much to do,
to save your soldier lying here?" But then
he's struck a blow behind his head and when
he twists to see this newer enemy,
a dread behemoth risen from the sea
of Satan's minions, then the soldier pales.
He tries to raise himself to fight but fails
to even rise up to his knees. Too late!
The giant demon doesn't hesitate
to drive his pike into the soldier's side,
then twist and yank it free. The wound is wide
enough to show a punctured lung. A roar
of victory escapes the demon. Sure
it's won, it turns to send its jeers across
the field. But then amidst this seeming loss,
the soldier hears a single bell-like call.
He knows that voice: the general! And all
the battlefield of friend and foe alike
is still as God commands His man "now, strike!"

And suddenly his part in this is clear.
There was a reason for his being here.
He was not simply left alone to die.
No, he was left to strike as if a spy.

The devil thought him done and showed his hand
but when one's called to strike, one need not stand.
So through the pain that causes him to weep
the soldier lifts his sword and strikes it deep.

He strikes and hears the demon's fearsome roar
turn to dismay. He strikes once more!
He strikes until his arm is hard to raise
then strikes again with whispered song of praise!
He strikes until the blood he's spilled is dry.
He'll strike until the moment he will die.
When lifeless hand drops bloody sword, its bed
will be beside the severed demon head.

So when this war of life brings you to where
you cannot stand or sing, do not despair,
but recognize the place that you are in
is right where you should be to strike at sin
and Satan's power. You're there with purpose, friend.
Strike deep! Strike now! And strike until the end.

Strike

Dear Readers,

If you are fighting in The Forlorn Hope with me, then I know that you have been wounded— not once, but many times. My own mind has begged an answer to the question "why have you forsaken me?" You have already read an entire chapter devoted to that question. But I have come to realize that this position I am in puts me in a powerful place to strike a blow for the Kingdom of Heaven. Let me explain. No, let me let C.S. Lewis explain.

In his book The Screwtape Letters, Lewis puts words in the mouth of a senior devil, writing to instruct a young devil:

> "*Our cause is never more in danger than when a human, no longer desiring, but still intending, to do [God's] will, looks round upon a universe from which from which every trace of [God] seems to have vanished and he asks why he has been forsaken, and still obeys.*"[5]

I, Dear Readers, am a fighter. And though these words do not stir my emotions like they would have years ago, they do give me cause to fight on. "But I'm not a fighter," you might say. I disagree. I think that beneath all of your fears, doubts, insecurities, and stains of sin, you are a fighter. Why else would Paul call us all to "Fight the good fight of the faith" in 1 Timothy 6:12? Whether or not you imagine yourself as a fighter, you are called to fight.

And to those of you who, like myself, are called in a unique way to share in the sufferings of Christ, to those of you who fight in The Forlorn Hope, keep up the fight! You have not been forgotten by God in His strategy. You have been strategically placed to strike a blow against evil. The Enemy may falsely believe that you have been defeated by the massive amount of suffering heaped on you — but you have not. So, strike! Strike hard! Strike deep into the soft underbelly of the enemy. Strike with the sword of truth, the Word of God. Satan's own scimitar of lies is raised to cut at the comfortable and those easy of mind. You are situated within the enemy's own defenses and can do more damage than almost any other.

You do not need to perform great actions or mighty deeds by any human standard. Every time you make even the smallest decision to obey your Maker in this battle, you thrust spears of pain into the enemy–an enemy who thought you to be easy prey but instead found you to be a deadly foe. You may not be able to see your effect, but I assure you that your enemy is reeling back in fear and surprise as your whispered words of prayer, simple kindnesses, resistance to temptation (mild or severe), and tiny acts of service stab and pierce his scaly hide.

I touched on this already in the chapter Gray Leaves when I called you to worship even when you do not and cannot feel like it. In this chapter, I want to point out that the worship I talked about in Gray Leaves does not always need to be formal, corporate, or private worship. It can be any decision you make that follows the plan and purposes of God laid out for you in Scripture. Remember this, if you can, when faced with your daily decisions. They are not meaningless or inconsequential. These choices are fearsome blows to the stronghold of the enemy. That battering ram I wrote about in the title poem is not just swung by famous men doing widespread works. It is swung just as hard by you choosing to offer up a single word of thanks to God in the midst of your daily struggle.

Caregivers, it may not be your place to exhort them to obedience in the same forceful way that I have here in this chapter. I am calling out to those alongside me even as I struggle to apply this truth myself. This direct style of exhortation may not be as well-received coming from someone in a different battle. That being said, you can serve them in this area by affirming and encouraging them for the ways that they do this already. Do you see them obeying? Let them know that they are doing mighty things for the kingdom of God. This will not only boost their morale for their struggles, but it will make them aware of this truth in an affirming and gentle way without the force of a command.

The Deeper Purpose

There's a mysterious transformation
when hurt leaves this temporal plane,
a process of glorification
that started here as pain.
Though for now, we cannot perceive it
since our eyes are not yet fully grown.
But there will come a day we receive it,
standing humbly in front of the throne.

So do not despair that you're crawling
down the thorn-ridden pathway of life,
though your everyday wounds are appalling,
and your rucksack is laden with strife.
Every drip of your blood is remembered
every teardrop is lovingly kept
so that someday those tears can be rendered
into beauty. You'll know why you wept.

Even pleasures are loss next to glory
and the promise is glory from grief.
Though your battles be savage and gory,
they're, compared to eternity, brief.
So remember that pain has a purpose
beyond all terrestrial sight.
The suffering here is the surface.
Beyond the deep darkness is light.

The Deeper Purpose

Dear Readers,

I sometimes like to throw off Christians who are unfamiliar with my thought processes by saying, "I don't think God always has a reason for the things He does" ... pause... "I think He has reasons–plural." I believe that God does everything that He does for many reasons that lead His people to the right path and bring them the most good and Himself the most glory.

I know that my Maker has many reasons for the things He does and allows, and those allowances oftentimes include suffering in the lives of those He loves. Sometimes, God allows us to hurt because it draws us closer to Him. There are times when the purpose is to teach us something about Himself. Still other times, it's to help us to grow in our ability to understand His love through sharing in the sufferings of Christ. There are many ways during this lifetime that we are served by suffering. There are many reasons for it, sometimes many of them mixed together. But there is one reason (one reason that I can actually comprehend, anyway) that I hold dearer and more important than all the rest, though I do not understand it fully.

This truth is that somehow earthly suffering produces eternal blessing. 2 Corinthians 4:17-18 says,

"For this light momentary affliction is preparing for us an eternal weight of glory beyond all comparison, as we look not to the things that are seen but to the things that are unseen. For the things that are seen are transient, but the things that are unseen are eternal." (ESV)

Paul doesn't go into much detail, I know, but the promise is clear. Somehow, affliction here on earth translates into eternal glory outside of the bounds of time and space. Now, there's one point I want to make abundantly clear. There is no talk of *earning* this "eternal weight of glory" (though that might be your first instinct to assume on reading this passage). The free gifts of God are not earned by anything that we do. Let's have no confusion about that. Somehow, our suffering "prepares" glory for us. It doesn't mean that we earned it. It means that suffering is the temporal tip of an eternal iceberg of joy. They are two parts of one progression, though they are seen as opposites on either side of the wall of eternity.

I am not sure how pain and glory align like this, but no matter the process, those of us who suffer ought to be heartened by this truth. This life is not the end and we will have more than just rest at the end of our long struggle; we will have glory! There will be indescribable, incomparable good that comes to us when we meet our Savior after our time on earth is done. There is an eternal purpose to the pain we endure here, and there is beauty and wonder that follows. The same God who paints the sky in evening and placed the stars in the heavens, who guides the currents of the seas and who commands the storms — this God promises glory to you "beyond all comparison" as a result of your pain.

Caregivers, this may be a good truth of which to remind sufferers directly, though gently and humbly. Do *not* say to them, "You're going to be rewarded in heaven for this. Don't be so depressed!" What you can do is remind them that this suffering is not the end-all-be-all and that not only is it temporary compared to eternity, but that eternity is going to be richer for them because of their suffering now. Remind them that the God who loves them and is guiding them through this is not only shaping them here in this world, but is shaping the next world to be better than they could imagine.

Stories

Your suffering's a story, friend, and stories open doors.
You never know when people might have stories just like yours,
or who might be impacted by the tiniest detail,
or who might be inspired simply hearing of your tale.

Be bold, my friend, and share your life of suffering and woe,
but also share the faithfulness of Jesus as you go.
Extraordinary stories are not easily ignored.
So tell it, and perhaps it will point someone to the Lord.

Stories

Dear Readers,

B efore I get to the story behind this poem about stories, I
want to let you know that I am well aware that it sounds
like something that Dr. Seuss or Shel Silverstein might have
written (in its form and meter, anyway). That was deliberate.
I wanted it to be comforting, familiar, and reminiscent of a
childlike openness. No one is ever too old for some of the
lessons to be learned from children's' nursery rhymes.

So, on to the story.

In the spring of 2014, I did something rather bold and
unusual. I posted an AMA on the website reddit.com. For those
of you unfamiliar with this particular corner of the vast reaches
of the Internet, Reddit is a message board (of sorts) and AMA
stands for "Ask Me Anything." I posted a little about myself and
my story and then allowed literally thousands of people to ask
me questions about my life in the form of public comments. I
publicly replied to a few hundred of these. There were ques-
tions about everything under the sun, from people asking about
my daily routines to wondering if I had ever experimented with
hallucinogenic drugs (I haven't). A few of the questions allowed
me to be very open about my faith. Now, this wasn't the main
point of the post (though it was on my mind, my notes tell me),
but it was an opportunity I was not going to pass up. I was able
to share my beliefs in God, His plan, and eternity with over two

thousand people. My story of struggle, pain, and God's provision was visible for a brief time to everyone who stopped by to read it. I received dozens of private messages and public comments thanking me for my story, saying that it was inspiring for them in their own lives and faith.

I am not writing this to you now in order to bring any glory to myself. Anything that went into the AMA was all from God. My idea, the opportunity, the strength to spend several mind-racking hours on my computer, it was all empowered by God. To Him be the glory.

Also, I am *not* saying that you must post your story of suffering for everyone on the Internet to read. I have an unusual and somewhat fascinating condition that opened this particular door for me. People are often lazy and have a strong desire to be entertained — and not all suffering is entertaining. But if you have a story that seems to fit a particular audience, it might be worth sharing in a similar vein. It's up to you. Do as the Spirit leads.

And while you have a different story than I do and you will have different doors in your life, the principle remains: suffering people have doors opened to them to care and share with other suffering people and perhaps people in general. This is one of the many reasons for your suffering that I mentioned in The Deeper Purpose. Now, I know that I am asking you to be open and vulnerable and that is hard — especially when you've been hurt. But when God presents you with a chance to share your story, and the story of His grace and faithfulness, I must gently but strongly urge you to do so. God, through me, was able to impact the lives of dozens of people (perhaps many, many more), pointing them to Himself. If you can do the same for even one person in your life, I believe that it is worth it.

Caregivers, I would ask you to encourage those who are already living openly and sharing their stories by honoring them for it when they do. Look around you. Who is living through their suffering in a transparent and open way? Thank them for their story. The thanks of a grateful heart is strength to a suffering soul.

We Are a Gift

My friends, are you the sort to turn away
the gifts of God? The pain he sends to you
and those among you *is* a gift. It may

not seem so, but it is. And churches who
reject this gift reject the ways the Lord
will often work in hearts like yours. So, do

you want to grow in kindness? Take the stored-
up strength you have and share. Do you desire
to understand the One from whose wounds poured

such saving grace? If so, you must aspire
to draw up close to those with wounds and share
in them. Go join your brothers in the fire.

You are one body — broken. As you care
for injured feet, well then, the arms must lift
the crutches and grow strong with strain. Beware

to those who do not seize upon this gift.
A body with a wound that will not heal
grows sick. A festered leg is cut adrift

and then the body as a whole can't feel
the ground beneath it. Do not waste this chance.
The good and cost of failure both are real.

Don't listen to your heart that, at first glance,
will quail and say "that's too uncomfortable."
This calling is of dire significance.

So if you care about the body's health
and want to grow its spiritual wealth

then find the ones in pain and when you do,
give them the same love Jesus gave to you.

We Are a Gift

Dear Readers,

This chapter is once again directed at the Caregivers — specifically, as you can tell, at the churches that surround those of us in The Forlorn Hope. While it is a good thing to care for those around you who suffer no matter their involvement in your church or any church, there is a special calling on the Christian church to care for their members who are hurting. "If one member suffers, all suffer together" (1 Corinthians 12:26, ESV). And it is more than a calling; it is a gift.

I do not think that I can expand on the truths of this poem better than J.L. Duncan. In fact, according to my notes, this quote of his, posted to a social media site, was what inspired this chapter. In his book, Does Grace Grow Best in Winter, Duncan writes:

> "Your suffering does not just belong to you. You are members of a body. Your suffering is for the body's maturing as much as it is for yours. Your suffering is there to build up the church of Christ. It is there for the people of God to be given faith and hope and confidence in

the hour of their trials. Your suffering is also the body's suffering because one of God's purposes in suffering is the maturity of the whole church."[6]

Do you see? Those called to live in a spiritual Forlorn Hope have not only been uniquely called to suffer with Christ, they have been called to share those sufferings with you. As you have been called to share your experience and understanding with the Body of Christ, those suffering have been called to edify the Body as they grow in understanding of what it means to walk through suffering. Will you wait until you also are called to walk through the fire before you begin to learn what it means to suffer well?

The apostle Paul himself laid out this principle clearly in Colossians 1 where he writes:

"Now I rejoice in my sufferings for your sake, and in my flesh I am filling up what is lacking in Christ's afflictions for the sake of his body, that is, the church, of which I became a minister according to the stewardship from God that was given to me for you, to make the word of God fully known, the mystery hidden for ages and generations but now revealed to his saints." (Colossians 1:24-26 ESV)

The suffering of the individuals within a church is a gift to the church every bit as much as it is a gift to the person suffering. I have explained a bit in the chapter 'We Know a Little' how I can see Christ through my suffering and know His love to a greater extent. I am grateful, in a strange way, for my sufferings. But Paul is clear. His suffering was not just for himself but for the edification of the church. I have

79

written as well about the call to care for those in suffering and even some ways in which offering that care can benefit The Caregivers.

But I must stress this: it is essential to the life and growth of a church to care for those among you who are hurting. The introductory poem to this chapter needs little expounding on this point, I think. You are being given a chance to vicariously share in the sufferings of Christ. Yes, it is painful. That goes without saying — that very pain *is* the opportunity. But it is more than just an offered chance. It is a dire imperative. You must care or die. The wounds of those who suffer are wounds in the body of the church that must be tended to or they will fester, rot, and people will fall away. If this happens, your church will end up crippled. Do *not* let this happen in your church body. Look now. Act now. Care now. My desire in this book is to help equip and prepare you to care for those in suffering so as to help you be effective in your actions, but you must act. Act in love, patience, and grace — but act.

To those in The Forlorn Hope, I will simply ask that you allow your church to surround you and share your suffering with you. I have touched on this before but I think it bears repeating from a different angle. Not only will a good church strive to serve you, but you will have an opportunity to serve them. As painful and isolating as life can be, your suffering isn't solely about you, it is also about the church. I believe that you will find strength and purpose in this truth not only to share your suffering, but also to suffer well. Allow the church around you to draw close and to learn from you and I believe you will be served by it as well.

Longing

Why do you smile?
Because I am dying soon,
and in death, I have a hope.

And what do you hope?
That I will see completely
what before I only glimpsed.

And what have you glimpsed?
Green hills rolling like the waves
and dawn that crests the mountains.

And whence comes the dawn?
From the blazing, loving eyes
that shine cool light down on me.

And whose are the eyes?
His, the One who made all things
and wears the form of a man.

And what man is this?
The God-man with nail-scarred hands
spread wide to welcome me home.

Longing

Dear Readers,

Lest there be some confusion, I want to say that I'm not dying any faster than most of you (I don't think so, anyway). I'm using the word "soon" in the same way that Aslan did in The Voyage of the Dawn Treader when he said, "I call all times soon."[7] In light of eternity, I will indeed die soon.

Now to clear up another question: why include two chapters in this book about Heaven? To which I will say, "Why not? Can one hope too much in Heaven?" There is actually some disagreement about this point. There are some who say that the kingdom is already come and we are to find peace, joy, and pleasure in that. They support this with such verses as Psalm 16: "The lines have fallen for me in pleasant places; indeed, I have a beautiful inheritance." And while I do believe that the Psalms tell us incredibly important things about God (who never changes), I don't think the perspective of every Psalm applies to everyone at every time. After all, the Psalms were written by a variety of people (often King David) at various points of life expressing different viewpoints of God. For example, not everyone is in the midst of crying out "My God, why have you forsaken me?" as was the psalmist in Psalm 22. Now, I believe what the Psalms say about God to be Spirit-inspired, eternal truth. But unless I am the most spiritually blind man in existence (which is a possibility), I believe times can arise in life where there is no peace, no happiness, and no hope in any pleasure this side of heaven. This is often where we find ourselves in The Forlorn Hope. I do not think God is wrong to place me in The Forlorn Hope. I know beyond the shadow of my many doubts that this is a good place because here is where I can bring the most glory to God. But in the moments of horrendous pain, exhaustion, and confusion, I cling to the one hope that I have left: that someday this too shall pass and I will be with Jesus. Sometimes that's all I've got.

While I am not shutting out the possibility of recovery or limiting what God can do with my life and what He can give to me in the form of blessings and experiences, I am not placing my hope in anything that is temporal or uncertain — anything that is not explicitly promised in Scripture. I don't know what God will do with my life before the end, but what I *do* know is that He will bring me home to Himself and there I will finally have peace, joy, and pleasure forevermore. This is the hope that keeps me going. This is the "coming dawn" that I have tattooed on my forearm. When I see that reminder to myself, it helps me to get myself out of bed in the morning.

I hope you are not in a place where you have nothing left to look forward to but eternity. But if you are, I want you to have the same beautiful hope that I do. I also pray you are never condemned by anyone who would say "you must hope for it to get better," or "you are hoping for Heaven too much." Perhaps you do have some temporal hope—and that is good—but you are in no way commanded to have it. Do not let anyone around you through ignorance or misunderstanding convince you that you are in the wrong to hope in Heaven.

Caregivers, please do not be concerned if we do not hope in anything temporal. We may never see an end to our suffering this side of death. Yes, we can be confident in the promises of God to find strength to face each day and to honor Him. But there is no promise in Scripture that says we will be healed, restored to happiness, or given laughter and and pleasure before the end. Do not ask us to place our hope in anything that is not promised in God's Word. You are welcome to hope in any way for which God gives you faith to — but do not expect us to hope the same way or in the same things that aren't grounded in eternity.

God's Love Through Sushi

I do not know that any life
is completely comprised of pain.
There are almost always little blessings
that, when properly perceived
provide a glimpse
of the goodness of God.

I see it in a cup of tea,
crisp bacon,
warm blankets on cold days
and cool breezes on hot ones,
a sushi dinner
with white wine.

God can still be good
and lead us through the fire
but He often offers balm
with tiny dabs of love.

God's Love Through Sushi

Dear Readers,

This chapter might seem to contradict the one before it (Longing), but I don't think it does. God doesn't promise that He will bless us in tangible ways in this lifetime, but that doesn't mean He never will. He has done so for me in little ways and I pray that He does for you as well.

I am well aware that there are those of you who cannot live a day without pain. I am one of you. I can partially ignore it, but I can't get rid of it and there are times when I can know, perceive, and experience nothing but pain. But those times are not my experience 100% of my life. There are little times of laughter and simple enjoyments that are touched by pain, but not entirely spoiled by it. These moments are precious gifts to some of us who suffer even if they do little to balance out the weight of our suffering. I am in no ways saying, "Be happy! You have so much to be glad about!" I am all too aware that for many of you, happiness is an impossibility. But I do not think that there are many of you whose lives are entirely devoid of things to enjoy, even if just a smidgen.

Take a moment. What do you enjoy? I listed a few of my favorites in the poem — and I am not surprised to find that many of them are food. God gave us food for our sustenance, but also for our enjoyment. I do my best not to consume food to excess, but I do enjoy my meals and delight in them the best I can. When I cook a steak dinner with garlic-fried asparagus and sweet potato fries, my pain is still there and the confusion still holds sway— but there is just a little pleasure, a smidge of "Hmmm, I like this." When I sip on a hot cup of tea in the mornings amidst my thorough confusion about how the world works because I can't remember the past four years, those little sips are nice in a subtle way.

These are God's infinite kindnesses to me displayed in infinitesimal ways. His love is the very thing leading me through this Valley of the Shadow of Death. His love is the motivation behind His plan in bringing me into The Forlorn Hope. But that same love is also why He reminds me that not everything in this world was designed to make me suffer. I am nearly certain that He has given you a few reminders as well. If not, I will pray for you all the more that God's love would be clear to you in your suffering itself and through the truth of His word.

When you do have these little pleasures, treasure those things. Do not discount them because they are surrounded by and coated in agony. Let them remind you that God is good and that someday His love will take you out of the fire and into a land where pleasure is not just an occasional happenstance, but an inextricable ingredient in every moment.

Caregivers, my advice to you would be to provide as many of these little pleasures as you can to those who suffer. As you draw closer to them, you will learn the things that they enjoy. Try to bless them with these things when you can. This will not only encourage the person suffering and show that you care but it will allow you to be a conduit of grace and blessing from God to them, a position that does wonders for your own soul.

I do not recommend challenging someone in The Forlorn Hope to "count their blessings," "look on the bright side," or any other oversimplified statement like that. It is nearly always going to come across as ignorant and patronizing from someone who is not intimately acquainted with pain. I think that the best thing you can do is to be a supplier of these blessings rather than an identifier.

Romans 8

"There is therefore no condemnation."
The law and the flesh's domination
is done. There's life to be had in the Spirit
of Christ, because of His restoration.

And if you have this life, you then share it
with Christ and share His Father too. Re-knit
and adopted into His family.
You may call him "Abba" as you submit

to Him. But we must still wait patiently.
Glory *is* coming, though not so quickly
by our time, but soon when it is compared
to being perfected eternally.

And this is *sure.* The wrath that Jesus spared
you is spent! And on the cross, He declared
once for all that you are *loved* and no thing
or person can shatter what He has shared.

But hold on — who's this written to? It's not
just something general. When Paul taught
this, he quotes a verse from Psalm forty-four.
It's for those people that this was wrought.

So who wrote the psalm? The sons of Korah.
They wrote out of affliction and in war
that they were losing. And in their distress,
they cried out to God, "Why do you hide your face?"

"Why do you forget those who oppress
us? Why are you sleeping? You do not bless
us like you once did. Do not reject us!
Do not deny the grace that You possess!"

See it now? The import is enormous.
Paul wrote this for *you* in your ruinous
suffering. As you weep and as you groan,
these words give strength in your tumultuous

life. It is essential for you to own
these verses. The truth and even the tone
are for those of us in the deepest pain.
The words of Romans eight are not full-grown

in someone's mind before their hearts have gained
appreciation for the heavy strain
of those in Psalm forty-four. Your deep night
is the most important place to ingrain

this. To know the life you have and light
and future glory that you share with Christ,
to know there can be no separation —
grip *this* as your sword in the coming fight.

Romans 8

My Dear Readers,

This chapter's poem may come across as a bit of literary criticism in its deconstruction of the passage. I prefer to think of it as a bit of exegesis. I love all of Romans. It is so packed with truth!

Romans 8, like the rest of Romans, is very dense. It talks about several different aspects of salvation and how they play out in the life of a Christian. These verses are powerful, intense, and complex truths that have a million applications. Paul wrote those words to the church in Rome at large — but I think he had a specific group in mind when he penned verses 18-39. He tells us who that group is when he quotes Psalm 44, "Yet for your sake we are being killed all the day long; we are regarded as sheep to be slaughtered." (Romans 8:36 & Psalm 44:22 ESV). The people who were living their lives in touch with the words of Psalm 44 are the specific target of those truths.

Psalm 44 is arguably one of the most forlorn of all the Psalms. If you've read through the Psalms, you know that they can get very dark, but will most often end on a note of hope, like at the end of Psalm 42, "Hope in God; for I shall again praise him, my salvation and my God" (verse 11, ESV). But when it comes to Psalm 44, there is no discernable hope or rejoicing. It begins talking about the sovereignty of God and about the faithfulness of His people and how God supported and strengthened them. Then it lays out a clear complaint to God: "But you have rejected us and disgraced us" (verse 9). This tribulation was not the judgement of God against sin. The sons of Korah write, "Our heart has not turned back, nor have our steps departed from your way; yet you have broken us in the place of jackals and covered us with the shadow of death," (Psalm 44:18-19, ESV). This sort of suffering is the suffering of mystery that I talked about earlier. This suffering is The Forlorn Hope.

The densely packed truths of Romans 8 are meant for everyone, but there's specific application for those of us in The Forlorn Hope. The sheep being slaughtered in this passage are the ones Paul is singling out here. The words of Romans 8:37 "No, in all these things we are more than conquerors through him who loved us" have special applications for those of us in The Forlorn Hope. As does "There is therefore no condemnation" (verse 1), and "You, however, are not in the flesh but in the Spirit" (verse 9), and "... you have received the spirit of adoption as sons, by whom we cry, 'Abba! Father'" (verse 15), and "For I consider that the sufferings of this present time are not worth comparing with the glory that is to be revealed to us" (verse 18), and so many more (all of them, really).

These are truths that you in suffering ought to read, think on, and own for yourself. This is the medicine that God Himself prescribes for those of us in pain. Now, I know there's a lot here. Perhaps I will come back and write more on these passages in some other book or blog. But for now, my fellow sufferers, I counsel you to immerse yourself in the truths of Romans 8 in the context of Psalm 44. I do not know which verse specifically will serve you. I don't know that you will actively connect with any of them. But I do know that it's a good idea and that it will serve your soul whether you feel it or not.

Caregivers, I urge you not to present Romans 8 as a remedy and think, "well, this will make everything better!" Though meant well, it will likely come across as naive and formulaic. My advice would be to delve into these passages yourself and delight in them as much as you can and then try to share that delight and awareness of truth with your suffering companions. Learn everything you can from Paul's words and then share them as best you can. Perhaps you could help direct their gaze to the inconceivable glory to come or the the Fatherhood of God who is Father to us all.

It *might* be worth asking those in The Forlorn Hope about their understanding of Romans 8 because of their experiences of life in Psalm 44. That would provide a context for them to meditate on the truths and for them to help you in a small way. However, this may only help some people at some times. Do not try this in ignorance of the personality or state of the person you are attempting to serve.

As a note of credit, I want to say that this was not originally an idea that I had myself. It was passed on to me by my mother, who in turn got it from one of our pastors (I don't remember which one). Anyway, sometime between the first time I heard it and now, after spending much time reading both Romans 8 and Psalm 44, the idea has sunk into my subconscious. I now cannot read Romans 8 without this awareness.

A Wordful Embrace

Sometimes we must fight back to back
instead of side by side.
Against this many foes we lack
a way to stack
our troops, but hack
with blunted swords against the black
and fearful evil tide.

Do not lose hope, dear friend, be strong.
I'm here though you don't see.
I've been behind you all along
amidst the throng
of right and wrong.
Please, hark my shouting, loud and long.
Take strength from hearing me

and knowing that you're not alone
though you might think you are.
Though our position is unknown,
we've *both* been thrown
here. Each our own
grave parts to play until the tone
that calls us from afar.

I hear your cries and tears my friend.
I hope you hear mine too.
But soon, I hope, this war will end
and happy then,
we'll melt and bend
our swords back into plows again
when pain is finally through.

A Wordful Embrace

My Dear Readers,

This chapter is aimed solely at those who suffer. You are not as alone as you might think. Now, I'm not claiming to understand all forms of suffering. I'm not saying that we're fighting the exact same fight. How can we be when we are different people in different situations? I'm saying that we're on the same battlefield. If you want to keep with the Forlorn Hope metaphor, we are assaulting the same fortification. We're looking forward to the same end of our pain and suffering. I'm encouraging you to realize that not everyone is ignorant of what it means to hurt and to hope for the end of that hurt.

There's nothing quite so infuriating as someone saying at your father's funeral, "I know how you feel. I lost my dog last week." And, I think, there's nothing quite so helpful as a wordless hug from someone who lost their mother the year before as if to say, "I'm here. We'll get through this."

While this chapter is hardly wordless (hence the title), I hope that it will be something like that wordless embrace. We're still fighting, Dear Reader. We each have battles yet ahead of us. But I'm here, and I'm fighting too. I hope these words will be an encouragement. I am sorry that I cannot be there in person to hold you, pray with you, or weep with you.

I suppose this will have to do. And someday, when this war is finally over, we'll meet on the other side of death and can rejoice in our Savior's victory together. One last exhortation from this chapter: pass it along. I cannot give you the wordless embrace that I believe means so much but, if you can, I urge you to find those around you who also suffer and give it to them. Sit down with them and encourage them by your presence. Share a meal or a moment with them and remind them that they are not alone. Don't compare — never compare — but do what you can to draw close and pass along the embrace.

The Smile

A kind word wrapped in grimaces of pain
is perhaps the sweetest.
Happy love is easy.
Smiles given through the eyes
above gritted teeth
mean so much more
than wide grins from full bellies
and sweet wine.

The one who showed us what it is to love
cried out amidst the agony
of crucifixion
"Father, forgive them."

We each are given smaller crosses to bear
smaller cups to drink
smaller pains to feel,
but we are given the same love
that caused a thorn-crowned head to think of us.

So when you see a smile
given out of pain,
treasure the gift of it,
knowing that it cost the wearer dearly.

The Smile

Dear Readers,

I wrote this poem while confined within the walls of a mental hospital. I don't remember my time there anymore. It's been a long time since I was there (thank God). But as I looked back through my notes, I saw that while I was there, I got a great glimpse both of what it is to suffer and what it is to see other people suffer. One of the things I wrote several times in my notes was that it was almost awe-inspiring to see other people in dark, horrible places extending kindness to those around them. People who were at their rope's end took a moment to smile and greet me. Now, I don't feel things emotionally, but if I could, I'm sure that my heart would have been warmed by their care.

To those of you who suffer but show kindness, keep it up! Not many people may know the effort that it takes just to flash a quick smile but those of us who do, love to see it.

Caregivers, I hope you can come to appreciate the things that those who suffer do and what it often requires of them to do so. If you see someone in pain who offers you a greeting, compliment, or even a smile, they are taking their mind off their own problems and battles and putting their energy into you. I hope that as you read this book and understand more about those who suffer, you will come to appreciate their lives and the effort they put into blessing you even in small ways. So when they smile at you, smile back.

More is Less

Two crosses sometimes carry easier than one.
The mathematics of kindness
do not follow normal rules
of addition and subtraction.
When in a time of difficulty,
often times the most relief
comes from shouldering the burdens
of those who suffer too.

The man who cannot walk
forgets his crooked legs
when mending the shirt of a man
with a broken arm.

Taking our minds off ourselves
and putting our thoughts on others
lets our own wounds breathe,
like changing bandages
to prevent festering.

Be sure to change your bandages often.

More is Less

My Dear Readers,

This is another poem that I wrote in the mental hospital, long before I thought of putting it in a book. So, once again, I must try to convey my thoughts about it at a much later time. Though, to be honest, I do not think that there's much that requires explanation. Instead, I will tell you a little about this principle applied — just today, in fact.

On the morning that I wrote this chapter, I spent time with a friend. He is a man going through his own Forlorn Hope. His life has fallen to pieces (not entirely through his own doing) and he is in a battle to find and cling to the grace of God. I am pleased to tell you that God has been very kind to him and that my friend is beginning to recover well. But he is still in pain. He is still plagued by fears, doubts about the future, judgement of others, and the weight of financial difficulty.

Over the past couple weeks, he and I have made a point to spend time together one morning a week. It has been a brilliantly healthy time for both of us. His troubles are not like mine but my own troubles and my understanding of God's love in those troubles have given me some words of encouragement and comfort for him. Being together has also allowed me to take my mind off my own burden. As I have thrust my shoulder underneath his cross alongside him, I feel no additional weight — and in some ways, my burden feels lighter. I am immensely grateful for this man and his humility in listening to my blathering on life and God and pain. He took whatever grace he could find from my words and turned that grace back to me which has reinforced my own strength in the struggle of my own Forlorn Hope.

Now, this is not always the case. Sometimes, you will seek to share someone's burden and they will strong-arm you away. Sometimes they will be rude, ungrateful, or even abuse your kindness. I am aware of this risk (and my notes tell me that this has happened to me in other situations with other people). I am not asking you to be foolish and throw yourself entirely into making someone else's life more bearable. You ought to know your strengths, weaknesses, and capabilities. Then, within those limitations, do what you can to give strength to others. It will do your soul good — that I promise — and it might just do your mind and emotions some good as well. Few things lift the heart as much as the smile of a suffering person brought out by something you said.

Caregivers, I have a recommendation and a strong word of caution. The caution first: do *not* simply unload your problems onto someone who is suffering without the camaraderie of a close relationship already in place. I know that it can sometimes seem like a good idea to bring up aspects of your own life as a distraction to those in pain, but without careful consideration and knowledge of the other person's struggles, the danger is that your problems could be taxing on the sufferer's weaknesses in a way that is not helpful. The last thing you ought to do is make someone's life harder when you can avoid it — and if you don't know what someone is able to bear with or what their strengths and weaknesses are, your wild guesses will most likely add to their struggle. This principle is not permission to increase someone's burden beyond their strength to bear. It will serve someone in suffering to be able to help someone else, it is true but, but you need to make that decision with care, wisdom, and knowledge and not before you have all three.

Now the recommendation: there is an exception to the rule of "don't bring your problems to someone suffering." Now, this is tricky and may not always work but when it does, it is a great blessing. Ask for help. This is simple, but complex. I have a few suggestions for how to apply this, though it will change from situation to situation. First, when you ask for help, make sure that you are playing to the sufferer's strengths. Don't ask a cripple to help you paint your house or someone with crippling depression to listen to your complaints about your crummy boss. But if you know that someone has a lot of knowledge (and the mental strength to apply that knowledge), you could ask for their advice on something. Ask a carpenter about redoing your kitchen; ask a man who is a good friend about how to be a better friend; ask a mother about any advice they might want to give you on raising your own newborn. If you think they can teach you something, it may be a good idea to ask for that. Or, perhaps if someone is suffering mentally and has a bit of physical strength to spare (be sure of this), you could ask for help with something physical. Personally, if someone approached me on a good day and asked for help splitting wood, I would leap at the chance. The principle I would recommend following here is to play to someone's strengths and lean away from their weaknesses. But in general, most people often like being useful and those of us in suffering are no exception.

Here, I think I ought to provide another example. I have a very dear friend by the name of Nathan. He's one of the few people who I knew before the accident who have stuck with me (off and on) through that massive change in my life. My notes tell me that he came over for dinner a few days ago and we talked for hours. I was so blessed by the time that I wrote it all down (as much as I could fit on a single page).

He didn't try to address me in my suffering. He didn't try to find the perfect words to say to make me feel better.

Instead, he asked for my counsel on something. He wanted to know more about himself and how to be a better man and Christian. He asked me to help him understand his own strengths and weaknesses (we have been friends for a good while, so I would know) and how he could build the strengths and wear down the weaknesses. He sat there in a brilliant display of humility and listened to me pontificate for hours. Then he thanked me for it as our time together drew to a close.

It was just the thing I needed. My focus was far away from my own suffering (though the ever-present pain had not abated and my thoughts were still jumbled). However, I was able to change my bandages in that time, letting my own wounds breathe the fresh air of grace that wafted through me to bless the heart of my friend.

This is the sort of example that I would recommend you emulate as Caregivers. As you get to know someone in suffering, as you begin to draw closer to them, allow them to serve you (in ways that they are capable) and they will be served by it. Now, don't *only* do this. This cannot be your only method of care. You must also seek to serve them directly in other ways as well. I can't give you much direction in this because it's always going to be very different for each person. But, once you have a bit of a connection established and you have shown through your actions that you truly care for someone and desire their good, I think asking for their help is going to serve them.

For those of you in the Forlorn Hope, please change your bandages as often as you are able. Keeping the focus on your own suffering without reprieve is going to only exacerbate the pain. When someone comes to you for help and you think that you have the strength and ability to bless them, please do so. It may not feel like it at the time (especially if your wounds are still fresh), but it will channel grace into your own soul even as you pass it on to others.

A Dose of Reality

Who needs more pity, they or I?
The broken or the whole?
My answer may well mystify.
For comfort's lie
can't catch the eye
of those who suffer. Amplify
the pain upon a soul

and then the devil cannot use
the tempting myths of ease—
since who in their right mind would choose
to favor views
of happy news
that all is well, with each new bruise
of life's unceasing squeeze?

No, we must face the fact that we
are broken and in need.
We have no place to safely flee -
except to He
Who Is. We see
no hope but in eternity.
And in that hope we're freed.

A Dose of Reality

Dear Readers,

I want to be very clear about something. This chapter is *not* an effort to give you a pat reason to be happy. I am in no ways saying, "well, you have this, so why aren't you happy about life?" The very nature of this truth means that to experience it, you are suffering— and therefore may be quite unhappy. However, it *is* a reason to rejoice in a small way as well as to gain an awareness that allows you to be better prepared to face the temptations that will come upon you. It is not a hard and fast rule, but it is often true that we who fight in The Forlorn Hope are not as tempted by the lies of comfort and complacency that often tempt the typical American.

When you are suffering, you cannot really be deceived into thinking that all is well with you. The Enemy cannot convince you that you need no help when you are clearly in desperate need of help. You cannot be fooled into thinking that there is no need for grace when your need for divine assistance is an undeniable reality of life. This is a clarity that many who do not suffer greatly will never have in this life. You must take advantage of it. You are aware of your need for help — cry out to your Maker for it. You are aware that all is not right in the world — pray for the justice in the coming day of your Lord and remind yourself that one day, all will be made right. You know that the world is a dark place — in that darkness, do all you can to find the light — it is often easier to see the glimmers of truth and love in the dark rather than in the grayness of ease.

Now, I am also not saying that we in The Forlorn Hope are tempted less than the common person. We simply face a different set of temptations (Caregivers, pay attention here). It is likely that someone in deep suffering will be tempted by some of the darker and more "blatant" sins. Often they are methods of escape: sex, alcohol, drugs, abusing food, abusing people, abusing themselves. These may be the more common temptations for someone in The Forlorn Hope. You who suffer must be on your guard against these things. You will have to make hard decisions. You might even be forced to make life-altering decisions to avoid such sins — the hand-removing, eye gouging that Jesus talked about in Mark 9 verses 43 and 47. Do not think yourself above reproach simply because you have suffered. Suffering does not make you a hero (no matter what social media says). How you act in your suffering is what makes you a hero (or not).

To the Caregivers, I have a few things to say. First, you must be aware that those of us who are desperately hurting (and are therefore tempted in different, perhaps seemingly darker, ways) are no more or less sinful than you are. We are no more or less saved. Please forgive us for our errors, no matter how terrible, and do not reject us because of them. Those of us hurting often make foolish decisions in our grief (though I am not excusing them). Those times are some of the most important for you to draw alongside of us and show us through words and actions that we are still loved. We may ask of the Lord, "Who could ever love someone who is as broken as I am? Who has done the things I have done?" Then, brothers and sisters, we must be reminded that love does not keep track of wrongs. Love is patient and kind. Please understand that we are going to struggle differently and that the best thing for us is to be shown the love of God that surpasses all understanding. If you must rebuke (and I know that there are times when you must), please remember the principles I talked about in 'Till Your Own Heart's Been Broken': love, forgiveness, and the meeting of needs.

Secondly, friends, I want you to learn from those who suffer. This is going to be a part of what I talked about in 'We Are a Gift'. If you draw close to those in The Forlorn Hope, you are going to be served by the dose of reality (second-hand) that you receive from them. As you learn more about how the world is broken and how the comfort that the world offers is a myth, you will be better suited to understand and meet the needs of those who suffer. You will also have more weapons in your own arsenal to fight against the temptations of ease in your own life. Don't let these opportunities go to waste.

Just Enough

Oh, Lord, you promised strength enough
to meet my daily, fiery trials.
What I must now come to accept
is that it is within Your right
to ask of me to spend it all
on what You have in store today.
My strength is not my own, it's Yours.
And so I'll press on towards the goal,
because I know that You assign
both strength and what demands that strength.
And if I must collapse in pain
when all my energy is gone,
I'll know that I have reached the goal
that You set for me all along.

Just Enough

Dear Readers,

There is a bit of irony in this introductory poem. I had intended to write a full sonnet, but I found my mind too exhausted to write in anything more intricate than a simple meter. It's somewhat fitting, considering the topic. I hope that this bit of writing exemplifies the truths contained in it. I have already alluded to the topic of weariness, but there is a specific pair of truths regarding weariness that I ought to address that have served me in my own Forlorn Hope.

First, God has promised to us sufficient grace. He told us that He would be there for us, and He will be — always. 2 Corinthians 12:9 says, "My grace is sufficient for you, for my power is made perfect in weakness." But He didn't tell us that His presence would make our lives easy or enjoyable. As you are probably already aware (and if not, then I am glad you are reading this), there is often grace that still demands our weary trudging in order to be applied. God did not promise us a surplus of strength. There will be strength, but sometimes (perhaps oftentimes, especially in The Forlorn Hope) just enough to get through the demands of the day. Grace could still leave us to fall down when the day is over, in seeming failure that we did not live up to the expectations we had placed on ourselves.

I know that there have been many days (even in the brief span of weeks that I have read about in my notes today) when I have set reasonable goals for myself and then rapidly become drained of all my strength, accomplishing only a fraction of what I set out to do. How could my efforts glorify God when I can only do a small portion of what I used to be capable of and some days only a fraction of what I think I am capable of now? That's where the second truth comes in. You see, God gives us strength enough to do all that *He* intends us to do. His ways are not our ways. His plan for us might be to pursue paths that He does not intend us to reach the end of, for we can fully glorify Him by walking as far as we truly can. His definition of success is not ours. He is still glorified by a warrior crawling with the very last of his strength and passing out from exhaustion, as long as he is crawling towards the goal He set before him.

Now, I am not saying that you must overextend yourself. You still need to be reasonable and responsible with the strength that God has given you. I'm not saying that you need to pursue exhaustion for its own sake. But when God brings struggles to your day that you cannot avoid (and this is inevitable in The Forlorn Hope), He will be pleased if you use all of the energy you have been given in order to do what pleases Him.

So, that is the truth of it. God *will* provide every bit of strength you need to do all he *truly* intends for you to do. And that is a comforting thought. It is not up to us to succeed or fail by our measures, but to spend what strength we have been given (perhaps every drop of it) in the direction that we believe God is calling us to go.

Caregivers, this may be a good truth to remind someone of directly (though always in wisdom and humility). If you see someone spending themselves in pursuit of God, even (and especially) in little ways, encourage them for it! Let them know that they are an example to you. Take time to learn from their example and let them know that you have. You might come to a place of exhaustion one day (whether that's part of a Forlorn Hope or not), and this truth is something that you might need to know and apply. So if you see someone exhausted, yet spending even a bit of their limited energy in pursuit of God's glory, thank them for it. They (like me) might very well need to hear that it has served God's purposes. It can be hard to stave off the nagging thought that we did not do enough or don't have the strength to truly glorify God.

Suffering Sovereign

Sometimes it's easy to see God outside
of the world, impassive and steely-eyed,
observing fire and flood and genocide.
We forget that long ago, He too died
a terrible death. Our Sovereign King,
Lord of everything, was crucified.

He's measured every drop of blood you'll shed
but not in ignorance — He too has bled.
He's walked down every lonely road you'll tread,
knowing what comes because He's gone ahead.
The man abandoned in Gethsemane
knows we are following where He has led.

Remember this truth, wherever He leads
you. Your captain knows what it is to need.
There's no price or pain or pathway or deeds
He asks of you that he did not precede
you in. The power behind all that is
is guided by His hands — hands that bleed.

Suffering Sovereign

Dear Readers,

This chapter is not wholly based on an original thought of mine. I have learned so much from the writings and teaching of others (Lewis, MacDonald, Spurgeon, and more). This poem is another inspired by Tim Keller's book 'Walking With God Through Pain and Suffering'. I have already talked a bit about God knowing about your suffering in the chapter 'He Knows', but this chapter takes that truth and combines it with another — the sovereignty of God. The truth that God is sovereign is not often a very comforting one to someone in The Forlorn Hope. We probably know it already and we might very well be unhappy with God because we know that He is in control. But to know that our sovereign God was also a suffering God — that is essential.

Keller writes,

> "We can easily see why children need to trust their parents even when they do not understand them. How much more, then, should we trust God even though we do not understand

him. It is not just that the differential in wisdom between him and us is infinitely greater than the difference between a child and a parent. It is not just because he is sovereign and all-powerful. We should also trust him because he earned our trust on the cross."[8]

Hebrews 4:15 says, "For we do not have a high priest who is unable to empathize with our weaknesses".

Your King is also your suffering Savior. The One who is leading you through The Forlorn Hope has also fought there — and died there. He is not a stranger to your pains, He is intimately familiar with them. He is not like a general in an 18th century army who bought his commission with family money and has never been on the front line of battle, sending young men off to die in horrible conflict, the sting of which he will never feel. He is more like Chesty Puller, a gritty Marine who saw hard action as an enlisted man before he ever got close to pinning on a general's stars. Your Savior earned your trust not just as someone powerful and trustworthy, but in the way that two soldiers trust one another after going through the same hell together. God's wisdom and knowledge of suffering is not academic. It is personal and actual with all the physical, mental, emotional, and spiritual factors that go into your own Forlorn Hope.

So what am I asking of you, my fellow fighters? It's not joy or even hope — it's trust. It's trust in The One leading you. You don't know where He's going. It may never get better before eternity. It may even get worse. But your King knows what you are experiencing and knows what He will provide for you and how to do that in an excruciatingly exquisite way in order to produce the most good. He knows the cost of it and He is willing to lead us in paying it, just as He paid the ultimate cost for us and for the glory of His Father's name. So, do not let your inevitable doubts hold sway. Do not let your fears about your guide have final say. Your God *knows* and He is strong. Caregivers, this is something that you might be able to directly but cautiously remind someone of. However, I would strongly recommend preceding it with the phrase, "I don't know what you're experiencing" before adding, "but Your Maker does." Humbly let your friend know that you are aware that you are not God. Don't just tell someone the truth of God's knowledge as though you too know what God knows. You might think that this is readily apparent, but people on both sides of the conversation need that reminder. You need to remember that you don't know everything about their experience, and the person you are comforting needs to know that you know that. Very few things are as repellant to someone in pain as arrogance displayed in false comprehension— even if it is accidental.

My counsel would be to *only* minister to someone with the truth that God is sovereign when it is paired with the truth that He is also well acquainted with grief. Only telling someone "Oh, God is in control," doesn't help much and should mostly be avoided.

She Lies

Oh, my young fighter so weary and wild,
weary from battle and wild in the eyes,
heed not the wooings of she who is waiting.
She smiles so sweetly but it is disguise.

Her face is a lady so comely and gentle
that spills out desires to "please stay the night."
Her lips curve and purse like the mouth of a bottle.
A taste of her wine is the promised delight.
Her necklace, it gleams like the point of a needle,
delicate, prompting the prick of a vein.
Her many rings shine with the glimmer of razors
offering bright and controllable pain.
Often she woos with the sight of the table,
gorging as if you could eat to forget.
Sometimes she picks up a clipboard and lab coat
and offers you all of the pills she can get.

But under the dazzle and sensual masking,
she's wicked and ugly and drools like a beast.
She takes and she takes so much more than the asking.
You pay all your life for the price of the feast.
Her fingers are hooked like the claws of a vulture,
her lips pursing up like the mouth of a leech,
she sucks out the lifeblood you're already leaking
from wounds you sustained in your fight at the breach.

Young fighter, I'm begging you, please do not go to her.
Turn back your eyes to the battle at hand.
You're promised the strength to do all that you *must* do,
but stray from the path and you'll no longer stand.

I know that it's difficult, fighting for so long
without all the comforts of hearth and of home,
and I cannot promise you pleasure or respite
or even that you'll not be struck down alone.
But do not seek comfort or temporal pleasures
from those who would drain all your strength from the fight.
Your glory and honor and Father await you
when victory floods all this darkness with light.

But I'll not spit platitudes then leave you out there
to wander away from your place in the line.
You're needed as I am, to hold our position.
I'll cover your weakness as you cover mine.
I'll fight right beside you each moment I can, friend,
and call all who suffer to stand alongside.
With hoarse-throated war-cry we'll battle together.
With shield-wall faced forward, we'll turn back the tide.

She Lies

My Dear, Dear Readers,

I t is no secret that war is hell. The spiritual battlefields of The Forlorn Hope are no exception. They are exhausting, wounding, frightening, and harrowing. They are often entirely devoid of any physical, mental, and emotional comfort. Sometimes the place where we are called can only be seen as good by the omniscient mind of God.

In the midst of these battles, there are many, many offers of rest, comfort, pleasure, and control that are promised to you in exchange for your strength. In this introductory poem, I have personified those offers of sinful gratification and godless comfort as a woman, tempting and inviting in different ways. There are the physical pleasures of sinful sex, the forgetfulness of overusing alcohol, the mental and emotional high of drugs and abused medication, the fullness of too much food, the illusion of control that comes with choosing to hurt yourself, and many more. This isn't a comprehensive list; these are just some of the more common examples. There are countless false promises of comfort used to lure us from the fight.

My Dear Readers, you *must not* stop fighting. Not for one moment! You are promised strength to face your struggles, but you must struggle towards the goal! Now, please do not hear what I am *not* saying. God's grace is not dependent on your actions. He will not remove His love because you have fallen into sin. That's rubbish. Do not believe that lie either. But God's grace is always going to push you in the right direction, and that direction is often going to be right back into the thick of the battle, right into The Forlorn Hope. It seems horrible, I know. I can't promise you that it will end in this lifetime. All of the promises that I can point you to in Scripture are for daily provision of grace and the promise of rest and glory at the end of your road.

But I can offer you this: I will fight with you, such as I can. Fighting alone is ten times as hard and we are one hundred times more susceptible to the wiles of the temptress. I have fallen to them myself at times (I mentioned this in A Mother's Tears). But I offer these words as a small reminder that there are others who fight, and I exhort you as a fellow warrior to press on.

I know the offer of my companionship is a little less meaningful coming to you from a page, but I hope it has some impact. That is why I want to call all of you in The Forlorn Hope to band together if at all possible. I know that pain is isolating and I know that you are all suffering differently (my own suffering is of a very unique nature). But, if at all possible, find someone else who fights in the smoke and darkness of the breach and stand alongside them. Find a support group. Find one other person who can in some way relate and seek to help them to press on towards the goal, turning all seductions aside as you pursue the end together.

Caregivers, I have already explained a bit of this in the chapters 'When Your Own Heart's Been Broken' and 'A Dose of Reality'. We are going to be tempted (and so sin) differently. Please do not judge us too harshly. Now, you must hate and revile sin wherever you see it, but please do not hate the sinner for it. Please do not cast us out because of the different sins that we fall into (not if we have any desire to change). Help us to fight back against them. Lend us what strength you can, even when you can't understand. Don't try to fix us, but try to point us to God who is the One who is able drive the sin from our hearts. You can't stamp out our sin yourself, so please don't try. It will only drive someone in The Forlorn Hope away and make it harder for us to remember that we are loved by God.

Outside the World Looking In

I didn't lock the door myself.
I didn't even step outside.
I only opened up my eyes
and I was here.

The window is too tall for me
to see inside, but I still try,
and every now and then
I catch a glimpse.

One glimpse reveals the happy day
my youngest brother turned thirteen.
I saw him blow his candles out,
then fell back down.

Another jump reveals the scene
of both my parents clasped in an
embrace with both their hair gone gray.
That's all I saw.

Another momentary sight
is Stephen's wedding day. The love
and wine were shared by all, but I
could not hold on.

Tomorrow marks the third long year
of jumping up and down like this,
with strobe-light glimpses of the world
that lives inside.

I wonder, is it worth it now?
To keep on mashing face to glass
to catch a single moment I
cannot recall?

I do not know. I guess I will
continue hopping like a fool
and misting panes to see the world
that still goes on.

So, if you see my freezing head
pop up outside your fire-lit room,
remember me because I can't
remember you.

Outside the World Looking in

My Dear Readers,

This poem isn't about a single, pointed truth about God or suffering. It's about me. Like the chapter 'Old Before My Time' and a few others, this one is a window into my own experience in The Forlorn Hope.

It's horrible, living without a memory. I can't remember anything past the accident — not for more than a few hours, anyway. I get a glimpse and then it fades away. The world has moved on and I have been left behind. I can't remember the 2012 elections in the USA. I can't remember moving into the apartment where I live now. I can't remember the past three Christmases, New Years, or birthdays. I'm pushing 25 as of the time that I write this and I can't remember being older than 21 (though I certainly feel physically older). I can't remember all the times I was with my family, good or bad. I can't remember the tears, the fights, the smiles, or the laughter. I can't remember relationships, events, or growth. All the memories that normally shape someone's view of the world are lost to me. I live in the past and even that is slipping away as those memories fade normally with the passage of time.

Hop — oh, look, Sam is a teenager... gone.

Hop — it's Stephen asking Justine on a date... gone.

Hop — oh, wow, Stephen is marrying Justine... gone.

Hop — my sister Mary is now engaged and moving to the west coast... gone

Hop — oh look, now Sam is getting his driver's permit and Aaron is a teenager... gone.

The only reason I know these things now is that they are written down in my notebook. I wake up every morning, confused about where I am, confused about the fact that I look different from the way I remember, confused about the fact that I am no longer in training to be a Marine Corps officer, confused that the world and everyone in it is three years older than I remember. If I could feel any emotions, I am positive that among the strongest would be the cutting sorrow and loneliness of living in a shadowy place, devoid of shape while I am aware that the world, my friends, and my family have all gone on living in reality. I suppose the inhumanity of being an emotionless automaton is a blessing in this way. But I still live in a world of confusion and shadows that pains my mind simply trying to comprehend it.

I know that it's hard to understand. I barely grasp it myself and even my closest friends and family only understand a little bit of it. I hope this poem has helped you understand a bit too. This is where I am. These are my battles.

To those of you in The Forlorn Hope, I am sorry that you must go through your own darkness. I am sorry that it must hurt so much. I wish I could lighten your load and ease your pain. I hope that God will use some of my words to give you strength as you battle on.

Caregivers, please remember what I have written here (especially since I have a hard time remembering it). Remember what I have tried to pass on to you and remember to seek out those of us who need comfort, strength, and help. We're broken, hurting people— each in different ways, but being alone makes it all so much worse. Please don't leave us here on our own.

The Forlorn Hope Reprised

The fight goes on and so will I
though I be weary and frozen.
And though I can't see sun or sky,
I'll choose because I was chosen.

Though broken arm turned wing is rent
the other swings the heavy ram
and He who gives me strength to swing
has promised me "I am,"
and "I will be," and "I will come again,"
and "I will stand in victory
above all powers and men."

That day is coming, this I know
and I will stand with Him
in perfect glory, peace, and power
bereft of every sin.

Yet here I'll be until the day
my battle ends in death,
but till then I will choose to fight
with every ragged breath.

Epilogue

My Dear Readers,

You have reached the end of my little book. I hope that in some way it has helped to serve you in your own Forlorn Hope. I pray that, somehow, my occasionally rhyming words have communicated truth, strength, and comfort to your soul.

The writing (and editing) of this book has taken over three years and I am glad to be finished with it. I can't remember writing any of these poems now, but as I read through them, I see milestones in my own growth as a child of God and as a warrior in The Forlorn Hope. I may not have an active working memory, but the effect of these truths on my own soul and subconscious has been great. They have given me much of what I needed to press on. They are proof that God is still at work in my life and I need that reminder since I forget so readily.

By the grace of God, there have been improvements to my condition since I finished the rough draft of this book (editing is a long and involved process). My memory span has improved, my energy levels are higher than they once were, and I am able to feel sparks of some kind of emotion. I am thankful that God has seen fit to allow me to heal a bit. But I am still not out of the battle yet, and even recovery comes with its own struggles, confusion, and pains. I am still with you in The Forlorn Hope and need to remind myself daily of the truths that I wrote here. It has been my goal all along to share with you the truths that have had such a great effect on me. These are not new ideas that I am sharing. I am no theologian. I simply hope that what I have learned over the years, perhaps written in a fresh way, will meet you and speak to you in your own Forlorn Hope. I cannot sit down and talk with each and every one of you. I cannot embrace you as I would like. I cannot weep with you and pray with you through our tears. But I have my words and I hope my written words have done what my voice and arms could not.

To those of you who aren't suffering in The Forlorn Hope but read this book anyway, thank you for seeking to understand and serve those of us who are in pain. I hope that I have not been too aggressive or demanding. I know that it can be difficult to understand and relate, but the fact that you are trying means a lot to me. The fact that you are seeking to be a better friend and servant honors God, and I pray that He blesses you.

To all my readers, God bless you. I hope to see you all someday when our victory is finally realized and our glorious rest has come at last.

Works Cited

0) In: Introduction
"Forlorn Hope." *The Oxford English Dictionary,*
Oxford University Press, *OED.com.*

1) In: Suffering of Mystery
Timothy Keller, *Walking With God Through Pain and
Suffering*, pg 205
2013, Penguin Group, New York
ISBN: 978-0-525-95245-9

2) In: Till Your Own Heart's Been Broken
C.S. Lewis, *The Great Divorce*, pg 97
1946, MacMillan Publishing Company, New York
ISBN: 0-02-086890-1

3) In: Promised
Timothy Keller, *Walking With God Through Pain and
Suffering*, pg 153
2013, Penguin Group, New York
ISBN: 978-0-525-95245-9

4) In: Let us be Good
C.S. Lewis, *The Magician's Nephew*, pg
1955, MacMillan Publishing Company, New York
ISBN: 0-02-044230-0

5) In: Strike
C.S. Lewis, *The Screwtape Letters*, pg 40
2001, Harper Collins, New York
ISBN: 978-0-06-065293-7

6) In: We Are a Gift
J.L. Duncan, *Does Grace Grow Best in Winter?*, pg 38
2009, P&R Publishing, New Jersey
ISBN: 978-1-59638-155-1

7) In: Longing
C.S. Lewis, *The Voyage of the Dawn Treader*, pg 138
1952, MacMillan Publishing Company, New York
ISBN: 0-02-044260-2

8) In: Suffering Sovereign
Timothy Keller, *Walking With God Through Pain and Suffering*, Pg 154
2013, Penguin Group, New York
ISBN: 978-0-525-95245-9

CPSIA information can be obtained
at www.ICGtesting.com
Printed in the USA
LVOW01s0004220317
528034LV00032B/727/P